MOONLIGHT
Abraham Lincoln and The Almanac Trial

MOONLIGHT
Abraham Lincoln and The Almanac Trial

JOHN EVANGELIST WALSH

ST. MARTIN'S PRESS ✹ NEW YORK

MOONLIGHT: ABRAHAM LINCOLN AND THE ALMANAC TRIAL

ISBN 0-312-22922-4

Library of Congress Cataloging-in-Publication Data

Walsh, John Evangelist, 1927–
    Moonlight : Abraham Lincoln and the Almanac trial / by John Evangelist Walsh.
        p. cm.
    Includes bibliographical references.
    ISBN 0-312-22922-4
    1. Armstrong, Duff, 1833–1899—Trials, litigation, etc. 2. Lincoln, Abraham, 1809–1865. 3. Trials (Murder)—Illinois—Beardstown. I. Title.

    KF223.A47 W35 2000
    345.73'02523—dc21

                                                     99–059606

Book design by James Sinclair

First edition: June, 2000
10   9   8   7   6   5   4   3   2   1

For my son
MATTHEW
with many thanks
for his unstinted help
over the years,
practical and literary

Biographies as generally written are not only misleading but false. The author of this life of [Edmund] Burke makes a wonderful hero out of his subject . . . so lavish in praise of his every act that we are almost driven to believe that Burke never made a mistake or a failure in his life . . . in most instances biographies commemorate a lie and cheat posterity out of the truth. History is not history unless it is the truth.

—Abraham Lincoln

CONTENTS

LIST OF ILLUSTRATIONS

This ambrotype of Abraham Lincoln was taken an hour after conclusion of the Armstrong trial. Of the hundred or so Lincoln photographs it is the only one showing him in a white suit. (Courtesy of the University of Nebraska–Lincoln.)

NOT TOO LATE

It's a low, sturdy, many-windowed old redbrick building of two stories. It stands on West Third Street in Beardstown, located on the Illinois River in central Illinois. Similar examples of such nineteenth-century official architecture are to be seen in small towns throughout the Midwest, many of them serving like this one as city halls.

On the second floor is a courtroom, also much like many others. A serviceable chamber, not too big, it has areas tidily marked off for judge, jury, prosecution, and defense, and a few spectators. Yet this courtroom, even apart from its old-fashioned air, is very different indeed, and the reason can be found on a bronze plaque fixed to the wall at the building's entrance. The Beardstown Woman's Club, it announces, "erected this tablet February 12, 1909 in memory of Abraham Lincoln who, for the sake of a mother's distress, cleared her son Duff Armstrong of the charge of murder in this Hall of Justice, May 7, 1858."

The mother's name was Hannah, and her distress over the plight of Duff, one of her six sons, was all too real. That Lincoln did what he did for her sake is also true, but the sentiment applies as well, and even more forcefully, to her unmentioned husband, Duff's father. By the time of the trial in 1858, Jack Armstrong was dead, which no doubt explains the oversight. Still it's too bad that his name, or some reference to him, was left off the tablet. It was Lincoln's memory of his debt to Jack, especially, and the dying Jack's pleading words on behalf of his accused son, that brought Lincoln into the most famous jury case of his twenty-six years as a lawyer.

More than that, it was a case in which Lincoln's emotions were stirred as perhaps they had never been before, to the point where he did something wholly out of character for him, manipulate the truth. The manipulation certainly involved witness tampering and the suppression of evidence, and may have involved the criminal act of suborning perjury. (This does *not* refer to what has become the best-known feature of the trial, an almanac supposedly altered in secret by Lincoln. That is another matter, also fully dealt with herein.)

A reputation for fair and upright dealing was one of Lincoln's dearest possessions, and more than a few times where the right in a suit appeared doubtful he actually withdrew. His friend and fellow-lawyer, Judge David Davis, said best what everyone knew, that "the framework of his mental and moral being was honesty, and a wrong case was poorly defended by him." To bring his full powers to bear, "it was necessary that he should be convinced of the right and justice of the matter which he advocated." Many others willingly testified to the same high compliment, leaving no doubt that it was true. The Armstrong case simply proves to be the one time it wasn't. Under the peculiar burden of an unpaid debt of honest gratitude, Lincoln showed himself to be no different from the common run of men.

Equally curious is the widespread misunderstanding about not only the case, but the progress of the actual trial. Even leading Lincoln scholars tend to get the essential details wrong, many misstating the facts of the trial's dramatic core: the moon's exact location on the night of the murder. Although much written about ever since in newspapers and magazine articles, for some unknowable reason—considering how every moment, every utterance of Lincoln's life has come under scrutiny—no one ever bothered to make a full-scale investigation (the present volume is the first book devoted to the subject, a surprise in itself).

In the absence of any close attention—the needed primary investigation—distortion was inevitable, particularly since there was little or no contemporary newspaper coverage. Inevitably, the few facts that were at hand became colored by personal memory and casual reminiscence. Lincoln historians, more concerned with their subject's whole drama-packed life, and depending on material already available, have repeatedly been misled. Harvard historian David Donald, in his masterly, one-volume biography of Lincoln (1995), justly lauded for its knowledge and insight, is only the most recent scholar to stumble over the Armstrong case. In his three-paragraph description of it he states that Lincoln, questioning the prosecution's star witness, caught the man in a fundamental error, claiming to have viewed the murder by moonlight, when in reality "the moon had already set." Not only is that assertion dead wrong, it shows that the writer has failed—as with how many others!—to grasp the whole drift and circumstances of the case, the actual evidence introduced in the courtroom.

There exist several book-length studies of Lincoln's career at the bar, and each of these naturally gives space to the Armstrong case, all stressing its importance and celebrity. One, published in 1960, *A. Lincoln, Prairie Lawyer*, by John Duff, supposedly offers the best treatment because the most detailed and complete, and has often been quoted. Actually, while it's a good try, putting in more effort than the others, it too lacks most of the essential facts, proving to be a pale, at times distorted reflection of the complicated reality. Earlier and later studies of Lincoln's law career—those by Hill, Woldman, and Frank, for instance—do no better.

One of the more serious oversights to be found in all prior accounts relates to the second man charged in the same crime, James H. Norris. Tried separately, and not defended by Lincoln,

Norris was found guilty of manslaughter and given a long jail term. That much information about him, along with his eventual pardon by the Illinois governor, is all that history has preserved of his part in the drama. In reality, though he was in prison two hundred miles away at the time, Norris played a pivotal role in all that happened at the Armstrong trial. Yet no real grasp of that facet of the trial has up to now reached print. The added fact that Lincoln while in the White House silently engineered the Norris pardon is also reported here for the first time.

Neglect of the case by historians was not because of any dearth of original records. Still on file in various courthouses in central Illinois are many of the pertinent handwritten legal documents, all drawn up at the time by the lawyers on both sides and by the court. They are not voluminous and tend to be skimpy in content, reflecting the usage of the day. But when studied along with other documents, the later statements of some of the participants, especially, they prove ample for a satisfying reconstruction of the event. Of course, much of the minuter detail is irretrievably lost, the precise circumstances of this or that action or moment. Yet, luckily, what is left proves just enough.

Absent from these primary materials is any substantial word by Lincoln himself (the only document in his hand offers added jury instructions). But present are statements, for instance, by the judge who presided at Beardstown (frustratingly brief!), one of the jurors, two of the other lawyers, and another lawyer who never missed a Lincoln case in the area and who was present at the Armstrong trial. Hannah herself contributes a lengthy interview, also a bit disappointing as to detail.

Deserving particular mention is one man, J. N. Gridley, a boy in Beardstown when the trial took place. As a young man in the 1870s his interest in the Armstrong case was sparked one day when he overheard two old-timers talking about the trial, one of whom had attended it. Gridley also came to know one of the jurors, and in 1910, after some diligent searching, he published a long article,

"Lincoln's Defense of Duff Armstrong." Gridley was a lawyer, not a professional historian, so his effort shows the usual defects. Yet it was the first sensible treatment of the case and preserves valuable material not elsewhere available and which would otherwise have been lost. It's a pity that there weren't more like him in those early days when information could be picked up for the asking—think of spending an evening or two talking with each of the twelve jurors!

Of course, there *were* a few who went eagerly in search of information, but none with Gridley's reverence for hard fact, even though his effort was that of an amateur. One of the first of the full-length Lincoln biographies, written by his Commissioner of Pensions at Washington, Joseph Barrett, was published in 1865, some months after Lincoln's death. To the Armstrong case it devotes no fewer than three closely printed pages, the text being supplied by an anonymous writer "who professes personal knowledge." The lengthy account actually proves to be perhaps the most inaccurate, overblown description of the case ever penned. Barrett's picture of the trial's climax is worth reading, if only to see how far astray it is possible to go in such things. Lincoln's whole being, says the admiring author,

> had for months been bound up in this work of gratitude and mercy, and as the lava of the overcharged crater bursts from its imprisonment, so great thoughts and burning words leaped forth from the soul of the eloquent Lincoln. He drew a picture of the perjurer so horrid and ghastly that the accuser could sit under it no longer, but reeled and staggered from the courtroom, while the audience fancied that they could see the brand upon his brow . . .

While the scene is pure fiction, probably few readers at the time would have been able to spot the excess, so obvious now. The modern equivalent of Barrett is the well-known film, *Young Mr.*

Lincoln (1939), with Lincoln nicely underplayed by Henry Fonda, if with perhaps a shade too much ambling. The Armstrong case forms a large part of the film's continuing action, though with all the names changed and most of the circumstances far removed from the reality. In court at the climax, Lincoln like a sluggish Perry Mason turns the tables on the prosecution's star witness, identifying *him* as the killer (he had nothing to do with the crime). Just as in Barrett, the exposed culprit with branded brow reels and staggers from the courtroom, now in custody of the sheriff. As an example of Hollywood's famous finagling with fact, the sequence is a gem.

A word more before we begin: it should be expressly and clearly understood that as the narrative proceeds—despite what may now and then appear—no slightest fictional coloring has been added. Everything said or suggested rests squarely on documented sources, as developed by close analysis and sober inference. Just to be clear on the latter point, take a small example.

In chapter three, *In the Courtroom*, describing one of the witnesses at the trial, I write: "Whether any of the jury noticed the look of relief on Watkins' face as he stepped down from the witness chair can't be said. If anyone did catch it, certainly its real significance wasn't guessed." Now Watkins' facial expression at that moment receives no attention at all in the sources, so it may seem to be a stealthy fictional stroke used for effect. But as the prior text makes clear, Watkins on the stand had quite ample reason for worry, and would have been under considerable stress. To Lincoln before the trial he had *said* as much. I believe that such facts give full warrant for showing Watkins' look of relief (with *that* much warrant, I might justifiably have painted a much more gripping scene!).*

---

* More standard historical writing might also refer to Watkins' state of mind, but of course with qualifications. Something like: "As Watkins stepped down from the chair his face *no doubt* wore a look of relief, *probably* not noticed by the jury."

City Hall

toric Lincoln Court House

The Beardstown courthouse and second-floor courtroom (the only Lincoln courtroom still in use). Today the building serves as the Beardstown city hall.

But I also make it possible for any concerned reader to separate hard fact from legitimate inference in the text. The extensive Notes section supplies complete source citation, along with detailed discussion and explanation of the narrative at all points. Since so much in these pages is new, or newly interpreted, and can benefit from discussion, I have not hesitated to make the Notes somewhat full.

At only two places in the narrative of the trial—Lincoln's exchanges with the witnesses Watkins and Allen—do I presume to detail what was actually said, though *without* the use of quotation marks (which of course are reserved for verbatim use of actual sources). My purpose is to make graphically clear and immediate Lincoln's courtroom strategy at a critical point, while sparing the reader the usual convoluted analysis of evidence (which, again, can be found in the Notes).

If the picture I give of this celebrated interlude in the career of an authentically great man is not quite the accepted one, I am satisfied that it is at least the truth, or as near the truth as we are now likely to get. To have come this far, incidentally, and still be short of that truth, turns out to be the result of one sole fact: Lincoln preferred it that way. To no one, not even his own law partner William Herndon did he ever speak of the case, at the time or later.

When my studies for this book began, a good few years back, I was simply seeking to provide a fuller, more detailed portrait of a memorable event in Lincoln's life, one that had long fascinated me. That the intended portrait has turned out rather differently— in one respect startlingly so—I must confess has left me somewhat bemused, wondering which is more in order for what he did, censure or sympathy.

MOONLIGHT

A singularity about him was that often and
indeed in every case that I witnessed, he said or
did some very peculiar things, or some common
thing in a very remarkable manner . . . usually it
came at the critical point of his case.

Judge Abram Bergen,
who attended the trial,
on Lincoln as a lawyer

ONE

KILLING AT WALKER'S GROVE

It was a few minutes before midnight, the last curved sliver of a three-quarters moon about to slip below the horizon, when Press Metzger arrived home. Pulling his horse to a stop at the door of his farmhouse near Petersburg, he climbed clumsily out of the saddle to the ground, then stumbled through the front door. Greeting him, his wife caught a strong smell of whiskey, but she wasn't surprised or even much annoyed. She knew he'd spent the evening with his friends up at Walker's Grove racing horses and drinking. But James Preston Metzger was a good man, a hardworking father of three small children. Willingly his understanding wife conceded him his occasional sprees.

No sooner was he in the house, however, than the woman saw that her husband's unsteady gait wasn't all due to drink: the flesh around his right eye and brow was badly discolored, the eye itself swollen shut. Moaning, he dropped into a chair, his hands reaching up to clasp his drooping head. To his wife's anxious questions he mumbled a reply that he'd been in a fight. There were two of them. They'd hit him with something. One came at him with a club from behind. The other attacked him from in front with he didn't know what. The pain was pretty bad. Coming home he'd felt so dizzy a couple of times that he'd fallen right out of the saddle.

Next day the suffering Metzger remained in bed and the doctor was called. As examination revealed, the injuries were serious, the skull being fractured in two places: at the back, and in front near the corner of the right eye. The following day, losing strength by the hour, with the doctor standing helplessly by, Metzger became comatose. The following afternoon, September 1, 1857, he died. He was twenty-eight years old.

Even before his death, the search for Metzger's assailants—both clearly named by the dying man as acquaintances from farms in the Petersburg area—had begun. The first was James Norris, aged twenty-seven, who had a farm of his own, with a wife and four children. Second was William Armstrong, aged twenty-four, known to his family and friends as Duff. Single, he lived at home with his parents, along with two of his five brothers and two sisters. Within days of Metzger's funeral both men had been arrested in their homes by Sheriff I. F. West of Mason County and jailed at the county seat, Havana, a small town on the Illinois River, to await the October term of the Mason County circuit court. At that time the regular grand jury would convene, when a decision would be made about charging the two. While waiting for the grand jury the authorities found that Norris had earlier been involved in another serious scrape and had been tried for manslaughter in the death of a man named Thornburg. That time he'd been acquitted on a plea of self-defense.

Both suspects came of old central Illinois families, pioneer stock. Armstrong's father and mother—John, or Jack, and Hannah—had been there the longest, reaching the state more than thirty years before, when the Indians were still an occasional problem. (As a young militia sergeant Jack had fought in the Black Hawk War, coming home unscathed.) At first, the Armstrongs had settled just south of Petersburg, near the small, struggling village of New Salem where, like all the other settlers, they occupied a rough log cabin. In the 1840s, with the rapid rise of Petersburg, along with most other New Salemites, they gave up on the dwindling village, moving ten miles north to their present forty-acre farm. The Armstrong sons, though rough-mannered and given to drink and boisterous horseplay, were all hardworking farmers and law-abiding citizens. Duff's arrest in connection with the violent death of a neighbor left the whole family in shock.

On October 26 in the courtroom at Havana the Mason County grand jury began its deliberations, the Metzger case being its most pressing business. During several days it heard testimony from witnesses, a total of ten young men, all of whom had been at Walker's Grove the night of the fight. Also testifying was Dr. B. F. Stephenson, a Petersburg physician who described the fatal head wounds, explaining how they had caused the unlucky Metzger's death. The picture that emerged of that night's embroilment was an all-too familiar one involving a lethal combination of heavy drinking and flaring tempers.

At Walker's Grove on the night of Saturday, August 29, a religious camp-meeting had been in progress for a week, drawing enthusiastic crowds from a wide section of the countryside (churches were still few in the area and camp-meetings lasting a week or two were the usual substitute). Tents and makeshift wooden structures accommodated those who chose to remain on the grounds overnight or for longer, and the inevitable horde of sutler's wagons offering food and drink had followed. These by law were kept at a distance from the meeting grounds, being allowed to set up no nearer than a half-mile. It was in the vicinity of one of these outlying wagons that the unwary Metzger met his sad fate.

As outlined by the grand jury indictment, and drawing on the eyewitness testimony, it can be said that the attack on Metzger was both brutal and concerted, though not unprovoked. At dusk on the twenty-ninth, with the horse racing ended, Metzger spent several hours drinking, at length arriving at one of the wagons where he encountered Norris and Armstrong. All three knew each other well, and while not close friends were ordinarily on good terms. Armstrong, who had also spent the day at the horse races and drinking, lay asleep on a bench. Metzger, a large and powerful man, in a fit of devilment caught Armstrong by the legs and dragged him off the bench to the ground. Dazed, Armstrong, who was much smaller and lighter in build, struggled angrily to his feet but offered his antagonist only a token show of retaliation. The two then had a drink together, Armstrong apparently calm again but in reality still seething.

Shortly afterward at the same wagon the bearish Metzger became involved in a similar bit of roughhousing with Norris, also a man of light build, leaving Norris' feelings equally ruffled. Within an hour of these two seemingly superficial altercations there occurred the incident which was to prove fatal for the marauding Metzger.

In the bare, legalistic words of the grand jury indictment, Norris and Armstrong "unlawfully, feloniously, willfully, and of their malice aforethought did make an assault" on Metzger. They didn't come at their formidable target with bare hands. Norris had used as a weapon "a certain stick of wood three feet long and of the diameter of two inches" (later identified as a "neck-yoke," part of a wagon's frame). Armstrong had wielded a more unusual though equally effective weapon, "a certain hard metallic substance commonly called a slung-shot" (a lead ball encased in leather with a cord attached for swinging).*

Norris' blow was a devastating one, delivered from behind. It gave to "the back part of the head of him the said James Preston Metzger one mortal bruise." At the same moment or shortly afterward Armstrong struck, either from in front or from off to the

---

* Previous writers on the case all mistake this weapon for the ordinary "sling shot," used to hurl a pellet or projectile at an opponent from a distance. The slung-shot was actually a sort of long-handled blackjack, intended for use close up.

Jack and Hannah Armstrong, friends of Lincoln's younger days, shown about the time they asked him to defend their son on a murder charge. Below: William "Duff" Armstrong, shortly after his trial for murder in 1858 and in later life.

side. The deadly lead weight of the slung-shot smashed "in and upon the right eye," causing the victim to sustain "one other mortal bruise." Together these two savage injuries caused Metzger to "languish" for three days, at last killing him.

On November 5 in the Mason County courthouse, as the two prisoners and their families listened anxiously, the lengthy grand jury indictment was read out. Carefully phrased to cover every possible angle of the crime, it charged the two men with first-degree murder. The penalty if convicted was death by hanging.

Lawyers for Duff Armstrong had already been arranged by his parents, the firm of Dilworth & Campbell in Havana. Norris had to plead financial inability, and was assigned counsel by the court, William Walker of the Havana firm of Walker & Lacey. On the same day that the charges were handed up, Dilworth & Campbell, acting for both defendants, moved to quash the indictment. In support of the action ten points were cited, most of them simply questioning the grand jury proceedings technically. Three went to the merits of the case: (1) Metzger's head wounds were not adequately described, (2) it was not clearly stated whether the defendants had acted in concert, (3) it was not stated which of the two wounds had caused Metzger's death. The judge brushed aside the motion to quash, rejecting it without comment or discussion.

With that, Dilworth & Campbell, acting solely for their client, Armstrong, requested a change of venue ("he fears that he will not receive a fair and impartial trial in this court, on account of the mind of the inhabitants of said Mason County being prejudiced against him"). It was an almost automatic motion, one that a court seldom questioned or refused, the grounds usually being more convenient than accurate. This time the judge agreed, naming Cass County, adjacent to Mason on the southwest, as the new venue for Armstrong.

Whatever actually prompted the move, it was a fortunate one. Had Armstrong gone to trial in Mason at the November term, as Norris did, he would certainly have been convicted, though perhaps on a reduced charge. Why Norris and his attorney elected to remain in Mason isn't stated. It proved to be an obvious tactical blunder, however, one that was strangely compounded by Walker's letting the case go so speedily to trial. On November 7, only two days after the indictment was handed up, at the conclusion of a one-day trial, Norris was convicted of manslaughter. The sentence, imposed by the jury along with its verdict, as the judge had directed, called for eight years at hard labor in the Illinois penitentiary.

In almost peremptory style had Norris' fate been decided. For the prosecution no more than five witnesses had appeared: Metzger's brother Grigsby, three of his friends (Charles Allen, William Killion, James Walker), and the medical expert, Dr. Stephenson. The brother and the three friends all swore that they saw Norris deal the fatal blow. The time was eleven o'clock at night, but there was a bright moon high in the sky, almost overhead, and the four were watching the fight from about forty feet away. Dr. Stephenson authoritatively explained that the fracture at the rear of the skull by itself could have caused death.

In Norris' defense it was admitted that the young man had indeed fought with Metzger, but it was emphatically denied that he'd used any sort of weapon, only his fists, hardly a threat to his large opponent. In any case, asserted the defense, no matter how hard a blow might be delivered by a fist it could not crack a skull. That injury must have been sustained later, perhaps when the dead man fell from his horse going home. All four prosecution eyewitnesses were challenged as having stood much further off from the fight than a mere forty feet—two or three times that distance, it was insisted, much too far for onlookers to be sure what happened even with a bright moon shining. (A check of an almanac had satisfied the defense that the prosecution was correct, and that there had been a bright moon visible at the hour stated on August 29.)

None of this was convincing to the jury, especially when they heard one of the four, Charles Allen, earnestly insist that he'd been much closer to the scene of the battle than the other three, and couldn't be mistaken. He knew Norris well, saw him attack Metzger with a club, saw the deadly blow inflicted, was watching as the stricken man went down.

With the rapid and decisive conclusion of the Norris trial, and with Duff's case about to come up in the Cass County circuit court at Beardstown, Jack and Hannah Armstrong had to face the alarming probability that their son would be convicted, probably receiving a sentence no less than that given Norris. If the Beardstown jury should prove sterner than that at Havana, they might even conclude to a charge of outright murder, and Duff could well be facing the gallows. The same body of evidence that had been presented by the Norris prosecutors, the same damning witnesses, would be involved. In addition, the Armstrongs now had to face the fact that they could no longer afford to pay for lawyers. After so many years of struggle, their little farm was all they had.

It was a few days afterward that a final, devastating blow fell on the harried family. Jack, ailing for some time, grew suddenly much worse, and by early November he was dead. Before he breathed his last he whispered to Hannah a heartfelt wish that his hapless son be saved. If necessary, Hannah must sell the farm to pay for good lawyers, the best that could be found. Who they might be he had no idea, but there was one name out of his own past he'd like Hannah to see about, a man they both remembered fondly, Abe Lincoln.

Twenty years and more had sped by since the Armstrongs had known young Abe in their New Salem days. Since then he'd come a long way. Now he was a big lawyer in Springfield, a politician known throughout the state, and getting set to run for United States senator against the famous Democrat Stephen Douglas. The year before, he'd even been mentioned for vice-president on the Republican ticket and had missed by a hair. Maybe Abe wouldn't really remember people like them from so long ago, warned the dying Jack, maybe he couldn't take time out from a busy life like

State of Illinois } Of the October Term of the Mason
Mason County } Circuit Court In the year of Our
Lord one thousand eight hundred and fifty
seven

The Grand Jurors chosen selected and sworn in and
for the County of Mason, aforesaid in the name and by the author
ity of the People of the State of Illinois upon their oath
present that James H Norris and William Armstrong
late of the County of Mason and State of Illinois not
having the fear of God before their eyes but being moved
and seduced by the instigations of the Devil on the twen
ty ninth day of August in the Year of Our Lord one
thousand eight-hundred and fifty seven with force
and arms at and within the County of Mason and
State of Illinois in and upon one James Preston Metzker

of their malice aforethought did make and assault And
the said James H Norris with a certain piece of wood
about three feet long which he the said James H Norris
in his right hand then and there held the said James Pr
-eston Metzker in and upon the back part of the head of
him the said James Preston Metzker then and there un
lawfully feloniously willfully and of his malice aforethought did strike Giving to the said James Preston Metzker

James Preston Metzker one mortal bruise and the said
William Armstrong with a certain hard metallic substance
called a Slung Shot which he the said William Armstrong

First page of the original grand jury indictment of Duff Armstrong and James
Norris for murder, specifying the weapons used by the two men in their attack
on Press Metzger.

his, must have a lot more important things on his mind. But Hannah must at least write to Abe and ask him for his help with Duff. Abe might remember Duff. He'd known him as a baby in the cradle back in that old cabin at New Salem.

Tearfully, Hannah promised that she would.

TWO

SEND FOR ABE LINCOLN

Arriving at his ramshackle, one-room office in a dingy building on Springfield's courthouse square, Abraham Lincoln
was a worried man. It was the morning of November 10, 1857,
Lincoln was forty-eight years old, and what might be his last
chance at a political career seemed to be slipping from his grasp.
The senatorial nomination he'd worked so hard to earn, and which
appeared to be his for the taking, was now in serious doubt.

Already in his career he'd missed one try for the U.S. senate,
though coming close. Then, just the year before, he'd lost out on
the Republican vice-presidential spot. Since serving one term in
Congress a decade before, his had not exactly been a sterling
record for an ambitious politician. At his age, judging by the
volatile state of politics, especially in Illinois, there weren't many
chances left.

The situation was a little weird. By a supreme twist of irony,
wholly unexpected, many of his loyal Republican colleagues were
actually thinking of crossing over and throwing their support to
the Democrat Stephen Douglas. It was the proposed new Kansas
constitution that had caused the trouble. Recently readied to
accompany the Kansas Territory's bid for admission to the Union,

it made Kansas definitely a slave state, effectively canceling Douglas's standard doctrine of "popular sovereignty" by which each state could make up its own mind about slavery. Taking everyone by surprise, the angry Douglas had broken with his party and with the democratic Buchanan administration, openly scorning the Lecompton Constitution, as it was called. In a calculated bid to maintain his power, he'd thrown all his weight against acceptance, and Republican heads were still swimming from the dramatic development. There were even rumors that the disgusted Douglas would bolt the Democrats and officially join Republican ranks. If that happened, as Lincoln knew all too well, he could bid his own senate hopes a final farewell. The powerful, popular Douglas would sweep all before him.

What he might do about the swiftly moving situation wasn't at all clear to Lincoln. Something had to be done, but what? Where would he find the time or the energy? Never had his law practice been so busy as it had been all through 1857, his most active and by far his most lucrative year so far. Besides Springfield he'd built up satisfying connections in all the counties of the sprawling Eighth Judicial Circuit. Riding the circuit, tending to cases in town after town in a wide swing through central Illinois, kept him on the road a good part of each year, which meant leaving Mary at home alone with the children. Not the best situation, remembering Mary's nervous, high-strung temperament, but for a Midwestern lawyer it was the price of success at the bar.

Entering the street door of the office building, he climbed the long flight of steps to the dim rear hall where he entered the office, took off his coat, hung his tall, black stovepipe hat on the rack, sat down at a table in the room's center and began the day's work. An hour passed, then there came a knock at the glass-paneled door, bringing the morning's first visitor. It was a man named Tom Edwards, also of Springfield, whom Lincoln had known for many years, in fact as far back as his New Salem days, more than twenty years before.

He wasn't there on legal business, explained Edwards. He'd come carrying a letter from another old New Salem neighbor he was sure Lincoln would remember, Hannah Armstrong. Poor Hannah was a widow now—hardly a week had passed since Jack's death—and one of her sons had gotten himself into bad trouble. Hannah had not known how to direct the letter (herself illiterate, Hannah had asked a neighbor to write it for her), and had used him as an intermediary, explained Edwards. Hannah said he could read it, and he had: she was asking Abe's help for her boy, the second oldest, the one called Duff. He was charged with murder.

Mostly about Duff and his troubles, the letter also told of Jack's sad passing. Not much detail on the murder case was included, only enough to make it clear that the matter was very serious. Apologizing for her boldness, Hannah explained that it was at Jack's own urging, his last request, that she was asking Abe for his help. She knew he was an awful busy man. If he decided he couldn't do anything, she'd try and find somebody else to defend her son.

Lincoln's initial reaction to the double catastrophe suffered by his old friend must have called up scenes he hadn't thought much about lately—the cheerful welcome he'd always found in the little Armstrong cabin at New Salem (actually just below it, at Clary's Grove). He was a young man then, rootless and pretty much adrift in the wilderness. How many times he'd found company at the Armstrong table, how often he'd slept under their roof! To Jack and Hannah he owed more, in a way, for getting his start in life than he owed to anyone else, Jack in particular. Good-hearted, powerful Jack, one of the strongest men he'd ever taken hold of in a wrestling match . . .

There was no hesitation. As soon as Lincoln finished readying the letter he said to the waiting Edwards that of course he'd help, be glad to do what he could. He'd write Hannah that very minute.

With that, in some diffidence Edwards brought up the matter of Lincoln's fee. As both he and Hannah anticipated, for such a case, and with a lawyer of Lincoln's standing, it could hardly be a small one, and Hannah had precious little with which to pay a fee of any size. She really *might* be forced to sell the farm to pay, as her dying husband had urged her to do if it proved necessary, anything to save Duff.

"You ought to know me better than to think I'd take a fee from any of Jack Armstrong's blood," Edwards recalled Lincoln replying, obviously annoyed by the talk of money. ". . . I've danced that boy on my knee a hundred times by his father's fire down in old Menard . . . go back and tell old Hannah to keep up a good heart, and we'll see what can be done."

It is the summer of 1831. The place is the little village of New Salem, a tidy, strung-out cluster of log-built dwellings. Along the single dusty main street, and in the one-room stores and houses dotted along its border, no man or boy is to be seen. Early that morning all the village males had streamed excitedly to the far edge of town where a bluff overlooked the river. There in the open space beside a log-cabin store, a noisy mob of men form a large, rough circle. At its center stand two men facing each other and stripped to the waist. One is of average height but impressively muscled. The other is tall and lean.

At a signal from a third man the two bend toward each other, arms outstretched. With both hands, each takes hold of the other's belt at the sides. It is all very formally and deliberately done. Then they remain motionless awaiting the signal to begin. The signal comes and instantly the two combatants take a strain on each other. Never releasing their belt-holds, swaying, turning, stumbling, twisting, pulling, lifting, every movement accompanied by grunts and grimaces, they battle mightily around the whole circumference of the shifting circle, neither gaining an advantage.

Minutes pass, when suddenly the tall man, every sinew and muscle in the long arms clearly etched under the brown skin, raises the other man bodily off his feet, spins him sideways in his arms, and dumps him sprawling on his back to the ground. Panting, the downed man stares up in surprise at his opponent.

"First fall to Lincoln!" calls out the third man.

A thirty-second rest period intervenes, which sees the shorter man surrounded by a large knot of admirers, all offering advice and encouragement. The tall man stands off by himself, attended only by one or two younger men who beam their approval of his performance. Then the third man calls the combatants back to the ring's center.

They bend forward, firmly grasp each other's belt, then they wait. The signal is sounded, instantly each takes a strain on his opponent, and the ferocious tugging begins. Round the ring they struggle, raising a cloud of dust, again with neither clearly superior. Twice as long as for the first fall they grapple, first one then the other seeming to gain the necessary leverage, only to be thwarted by the other's strength or skill. Then from the cheering mob comes a sudden mutter of alarm when it appears that the tall man has his opponent off-balance and on the verge of a second defeat. That would give him victory in the best-of-three-falls match.

It didn't happen. Instead of going down, the shorter man suddenly frees one hand, then reaches down and grabs one of his opponent's long legs—a clear violation of the rules under which the two had agreed to meet. Yanking at the belt with one hand while lifting the leg with the other, he attempts to lever the tall man off his feet and for an instant seems to succeed.

That didn't happen either, for the tall man as he is going down also proceeds to break the rules. In one violent motion he regains his feet and flings an arm around his opponent's neck, tightening it in a disabling choke hold. Sputtering, gagging, letting off an occasional bellow, the shorter man tries to fight free but finds himself helpless in the other's iron grip.

No longer is it a formal wrestling match. It's on the verge of becoming an ugly, no-holds-barred fight in which real physical damage can be inflicted. Blood might flow. With that, the mob surges forward, rushing to the aid of its champion, intent on sparing him further indignity, also meaning to teach the tall challenger that the Clary's Grove crowd isn't to be trifled with. In response, the tall man, releasing his hold, backs away until he feels the wall of the cabin behind him. "Come on!" he shouts, facing his attackers. "I'll take you all on! One at a time unless you're a pack of cowards." Ignoring the challenge, the stern-faced mob continues its advance, obviously bent on giving its cornered target at least a good battering.

"All right, boys, that's enough. Let him be." The other wrestler, his voice lifted commandingly above the rumble of noise, pushes his way in among the crowd, one hand tenderly rubbing his neck. "I fouled him first. Guess I knew I'd never beat him fair." Walking up to his surprised opponent he offers his hand, which the other promptly grasps, a smile spreading across the angular, clean-shaven features.

Slapping each other's back, exchanging gruff compliments, the two break into loud laughter, and the whole mob, after a moment's uncertainty, joins merrily in. For the first time in memory their leader, the renowned Jack Armstrong, the most feared wrestler in five counties, has been downed, fairly put on his back in the dirt, unofficially beaten (you couldn't say he'd lost, for the match hadn't gone to a finish). Yet here he is, treating his conqueror as if he were an old friend! What was good enough for Jack was good enough for them. A thicket of work-roughened hands reaches to extend a welcome to the relieved young battler.

Never would Lincoln forget the day of his epic battle with Armstrong—not for the excitement of the bout, not for the sweet taste of victory (no one doubted what the outcome would have been, least of all Jack), not for the satisfaction of having remained unbeaten as a wrestler. What mattered was the dramatic change in

John T. Brady, one of the Armstrong jurors whose letter preserves the crucial testimony of Nelson Watkins, an eyewitness to the killing. Below: Henry Shaw, prosecuting attorney and friend of Lincoln who assisted Prosecutor Hugh Fullerton in the trial. Shaw was the last owner of the weapon used by Duff.

his young life the match brought about, a change that came as a direct result of the acceptance he earned among the Clary's Grove boys, and because of them in the whole region. When he'd first come to New Salem, a couple of months before the match, as he often afterwards said, he'd been little more than "a piece of floating driftwood." The bout at New Salem was his "turning point," as he termed it when talking in later years to interested friends.

How different things might have been had the defeated Jack reacted, not in comradeship and good humor, but in anger and resentment! As it was, the outcome brought Lincoln, a few months after, election as a captain of militia in the Black Hawk War, the Clary's Grove boys with other New Salemites providing the necessary vote. (Even after winning the presidential nomination in 1860 he could still say in simple candor that his Black Hawk captaincy was "a success which gave me more pleasure than any I have had since.") That honor in turn opened his way into politics, everyone insisting that he put himself up for the state legislature. The captaincy brought him respect, admiration, encouragement, and loyal friends, especially Jack Armstrong—who served as a sergeant in Lincoln's company—and his pleasant young wife (Hannah had then just turned twenty). Though Lincoln lived in New Salem where he worked as a general store clerk, the humble Armstrong cabin at Clary's Grove and its growing family became his emotional refuge in those uncertain early years.

He'd drop by for a few days now and then, helping Jack in the fields or repairing something. Beside the fire in the cabin he'd talk with Hannah, and while waiting for some of her delicious cornbread to bake, he'd help a little by watching the couple's latest infant, rocking the cradle. In 1833 the baby in the cradle was a boy named William, from his birth called nothing but Duff.

Promptly on receiving Lincoln's letter, Hannah came to Springfield for a meeting, which must have been an unusually emotional
one, with much talk of the departed Jack. For reminiscing, however, there would have been little time. While no date had been set
for the trial at Beardstown, if it were to take place at the November
term of court, as scheduled, it couldn't be far off, a couple of weeks
at most. Little enough time to prepare a defense against a murder
charge. What Hannah was able to tell him, as she'd heard the
details from her imprisoned son, and at Havana during the Norris
trial, at least made a start. By mid-November the two had con-
ferred at length, and Lincoln quickly saw that the case was by no
means a simple one. In fact, it was all but outside his professional
competence.

While Lincoln was by that time acknowledged to be among the
ablest lawers in Illinois, his reputation had been made with civil
cases. At criminal law he was relatively inexperienced. In his
twenty-plus years as a lawyer he'd handled quite a large number of
civil actions, well over four thousand, many of them of course
being quite small. Of his few hundred criminal cases, barely a
dozen concerned the crime of murder. Half of these he lost, with
two of the defendants being sentenced to death by hanging and the
other four receiving lengthy jail terms. In none of the dozen had he
shown any special or marked ability at criminal pleading.

There had indeed been one curious, not to say strange case
which exhibited what might be styled his willingness in some circumstances to embrace unorthodox means. In October 1857,
only a month before Tom Edwards' visit to his office, he took
another murder case, a woman accused of killing her husband.
In it he displayed no particular legal ability, for the case never
reached trial. The very morning it was scheduled to begin, Lincoln
actually helped the woman to escape. At least the facts point that
way.

The woman, Melissa Goings, was seventy years old. Her husband, Roswell, seven years older and rather infirm, was a rough,

hard-drinking, quarrelsome farmer. In April 1857, in the course of one drunken dispute, he grabbed his wife by the throat, apparently intent on harming her. She broke free, picked up a length of wood, and when he came at her again hit him twice on the head. He died four days later from a fractured skull. There resulted much public excitement, with all the sentiment in the wife's favor. At Metamora in October 1857 the trial came up. The morning it was to start, Lincoln requested a few minutes to confer with his client in private in a downstairs room of the courthouse. Some time later he came back into court alone, and when asked where the prisoner was replied that he'd left her downstairs in custody of the sheriff. Downstairs she was nowhere to be found, and the sheriff could not account for her disappearance. A search was started, but was soon given up. The woman was never located, and eventually the case was officially wiped from the books.

Much talk followed as to what had really happened, with Lincoln being given credit for the lady's vanishment, though many concluded that he'd acted "with the tacit approval of the law enforcement officers." From the judge on down, it seems, no one had the stomach for prosecuting the elderly Mrs. Goings, and the dilemma had been left to Lincoln to solve.

His most recent murder case, one that had actually gone to trial, occurred just a year before, in November 1856 at Springfield. It involved another husband-killing, one George Anderson, who had apparently been clubbed to death, though poison was also suspected. Lincoln represented the defendants, the wife and nephew of the dead man, not on his own but as one of a team of three lawyers. The trial lasted ten days and caused a sensation that was reported daily in the newspapers, the *Illinois State Journal* regularly giving it a half page. Lincoln took an active part in the presentation, but the closing argument for the defense was given by one of the other lawyers. The verdict for both defendants was not guilty.

During the five years previous to the Anderson case, Lincoln had handled only four other murders, all of them on his own or as lead counsel. In each he lost, his client being convicted of manslaughter, with sentences of ten years in the penitentiary given to each. Once he was on the other side, acting as assistant to the prosecutor, for him an unfamiliar position. In that one the defendant gained his freedom on a plea of insanity, apparently among the first murder defendants to use that argument.

Preparation for the Armstrong case required Lincoln to push aside all other business, professional and political (the widespread notion that he made no special preparation but merely showed up in Beardstown the evening before the trial, spent the night in study, then next day saved young Duff, is among the sillier parts of the legend). Certainly he went to Walker's Grove to inspect the scene of the crime, and at least once he made the trip over to Beardstown to confer with the imprisoned Duff. He also went at least once to Havana to consult the court papers in the Norris trial. Of the minute-by-minute court proceedings in that action there existed no actual transcript—trial procedure then didn't call for one—but in its place he had the benefit of detailed notes made by William Walker, the Norris attorney. One other document also helped, a four-page, generalized report on the Norris trial and conviction, prepared at the request of the Cass County prosecutor who would be handling the Armstrong case.

A week's intensive study, however, brought an unexpected and disturbing result: it very much appeared that the Mason County grand jury had read the evidence correctly, and that Duff was indeed guilty as charged. The case against him loomed every bit as damning as had the case against Norris, the evidence being identical in each. If eyewitness testimony meant anything, in fact it was nearly overwhelming. Later, the judge in the case would recall how "Lincoln believed that the principal [prosecution] witness was true," though not saying what made him so sure. The opposing counsel in the trial, Henry Shaw, also later remarked on how Lincoln was all too aware that "the evidence bore heavily upon his client." Depending on how many of Duff's neighbors he talked with, he would also have discovered that among many who knew him the young man's guilt was scarcely questioned.

Almost beyond a doubt, the inebriated young man had delivered one of the two blows that had killed Metzger. That meant he *had* used the slung-shot, and not his fist, as he declared over and over, taking the same position as Norris in admitting the fight while denying the use of a weapon. It also meant that he had acted deliberately and almost certainly in concert with the other attacker. The two, after being rousted by the bull-like Metzger, had armed themselves and together waited their chance. Why they carried out their assault more or less in the open, and under a bright moon, allowing witnesses to see what happened, was an obvious question. Certainly it pointed to the possibility that some, at least, of the eyewitnesses knew what was coming—not a killing, but a beating of the big man by his two much smaller victims.

For perhaps the only time in his career at the bar Lincoln found himself in the excruciating position of *having* to defend a client he thought guilty, a cause in which he didn't believe. In the past he'd encountered similar situations, but they had been fairly easily solved, though not without serious pondering: he'd simply pull out of the case. If he tried to plead on behalf of evidence in which he didn't believe, he'd explain, all in the courtroom would spot his hesitation, all would be able to read his own doubt. No one would believe him, least of all the jury. In such cases his first effort would always be to advise his client that, if possible, he settle. Failing that, he'd remove himself. "He couldn't make black look white," explained Judge Bergen, a spectator at many Lincoln trials. "He would not intentionally misrepresent either law or facts, or use false logic. Some men think that a perfect lawyer can win any case, good or bad, and measure his ability by his success in securing victory for the wrong. Lincoln had none of this . . . if from preliminary investigation he could see that the law or the facts were against his client, a settlement was recommended. If this was impossible, Lincoln usually managed to get out of trying the case." If, as happened now and then, added Bergen, he found himself in the position of actually defending suspect evidence, "he appeared very weak, spiritless and destitute of resources."

But from the Armstrong case he *couldn't* withdraw. Not with all those memories of New Salem flashing through his brain. Not with the earnest words of the dying Jack filling his ears, the one man, rough-hewn as he was, who'd made such a difference in his young life. Not with Hannah praying at home for her boy to be sent back to her . . .

Truly, for Lincoln the situation presented a stark dilemma of a sort that, so far as is known, he'd never previously had to face in his practice. Rigidly opposing his natural instinct for right and truth there loomed the stern demand of personal obligation, a self-confessed debt of honor, always for Lincoln a sacred matter. In the circumstances his decision was perhaps inevitable, his reasoning of course taking the expected form (reasoning he had always before in questionable cases been able to resist): yes, on the evidence Duff's guilt did appear to be a fact, guilt made practically certain by the parallel Norris conviction. But who was *he* to make or concur in that judgment! Did he, a lawyer, have any personal right to say that young Armstrong was guilty? He wasn't a member of any jury, charged with the responsibility of deciding in such crucial matters. When a client claiming innocence came to him for help *his* business was to defend that client with every means at his disposal . . .

His painful decision reached, the only remaining question facing Lincoln concerned himself, his own inner reaction. Pleading for the acquittal of a man whom in his heart he believed culpable—a situation in which he was always at his weakest—how would he perform? About that, even he couldn't be sure.

For the prosecution it was a strong case, certainly. But perhaps after all it was not unassailable—not with one of the two attackers already convicted separately of the crime. The more he thought about the matter of the two wounds to the skull, and the conviction of Norris, the more he felt that he might have an opening for the defense. The Norris jury had agreed with the medical expert that the fracture at the rear of the skull had been sufficient to cause death. The wound to the bony framework of the right brow-ridge and eye socket might or might not have contributed to that result. Supposing it could be established that the fracture at the skull's front had also been caused by the single blow at the rear, the one blow having a double effect? Next morning Lincoln began studying anatomy books and talking with local doctors.

A second important element of the developing defense argument concerned the slung-shot supposedly used by Duff. It was a fact accidentally discovered by Lincoln in talking with the young suspect's friends that the weapon didn't actually belong to Duff. It was homemade, the property of Nelson Watkins of Menard County, who had brought it with him to Walker's Grove on the fatal night. Immediately on learning this, Lincoln contacted Watkins and asked if he would come down to Springfield to aid in Duff's defense. A farmer, aged thirty-four, Watkins readily complied, arriving at Lincoln's office a day or two later. What he had to tell, however, proved unexpectedly troubling, bringing Lincoln face to face with perhaps the most anxious moment of his life till then.

Watkins actually began by warning that Lincoln should *not* use him as a witness, adding in some hesitation that "he knew too much." Stumblingly, he went on to unfold what that "too much" really meant, only to have Lincoln cut him off. All he wanted from Watkins, he directed, were the answers to two specific questions. As recalled by Watkins they were: "Did you make that slung-shot? Did Duff Armstrong ever have it in his possession?"*

---

* All quotations in the Watkins-Lincoln interview are from the Brady letter: see the Notes and Appendix A.

To the first question Watkins replied with a firm *yes*. He had definitely made it himself and could prove it. There he halted, apparently unable or unwilling to reply to Lincoln's second question.

The weapon itself, Lincoln was aware, had soon been retrieved, found by the sheriff several days afterward near the scene of the crime. How had it gotten there, he asked. Had it been in Watkins' hands all night? Had he at any time misplaced it?

Subtly if noticeably, Watkins' reply as he later recalled it actually failed to answer Lincoln's question about Duff having the weapon, while strongly implying that he *couldn't* have had it. So carefully, so deftly is the answer framed—in sheer contradiction of what else Watkins told Lincoln at their meeting—that it can be seen as transparently a product of Lincoln's coaching. How much was pure invention, how much the truth, is hard to decide. It is a crucial question, of course, since on it hangs the decision as to whether Lincoln can be charged with suborning perjury in relation to Watkins' sworn testimony.

One of the things that Lincoln in talking with the witness in his Springfield office "would not allow" Watkins to tell about (the words are Watkins' own) was precisely the slung-shot and its whereabouts on the night of the crime. Watkins' comments on exactly that topic can be clearly read in the Brady letter: ". . . he questioned him about the slung-shot, and asked how it happened to be lost, and then found near the spot where Metzger was killed." If those were Lincoln's actual words, or close to them, they tend strongly to support the suspicion that the lawyer was deftly feeding his witness: he wanted a story that would keep the weapon well away from the angry Armstrong's hands that night, at least until after moonset. Watkins promptly supplied it.

Like all the rest of the carousing bunch, he admitted, he'd done some drinking. About nine or ten o'clock he'd felt tired and had crawled under a wagon to sleep for a while. He remembered that he'd rested the slung-shot with some other things atop a part of the wagon's undercarriage. On waking up somewhat later he'd forgotten all about the weapon and had left it there. In the morning when the wagon was driven away, he suggested, it must have fallen off the wagon frame and landed where it was found by the sheriff.

The little tableau filled the bill nicely, and probably at some time in the late hours of the twenty-ninth Watkins really did flop wearily down under a wagon. But his so conveniently leaving the slung-shot behind, and in a spot that was out of everyone's reach, is a claim that needs some faith to accept. Add the final item—the weapon supposedly dropping off the moving wagon near the crime site—and perhaps even faith is not enough.

Did Lincoln, building on some offhand remark by Watkins, simply invent the weapon-under-the-wagon tale, persuading Watkins to collude in it? Did he know when and how Armstrong really got hold of the deadly slung-shot? Did Watkins know? Did he tell or hint at it to Lincoln? Settling such questions requires direct, hard evidence, of course, so it must be admitted that no definite conclusions as to the suborning of perjury are possible. Still, only a die-hard Lincoln fan will refuse to concede that in these very peculiar doings there is more than a likelihood that the harried, anxious lawyer actually did cross the line.

Expressing his satisfaction with Watkins reply, Lincoln said that he wanted Watkins to testify at the trial. He'd put him on the stand for the defense and he need only explain about the slung-shot. All he had to do was tell his simple story to the court just as he'd told it there in the office, not a word more, not a word less.

Plainly uncomfortable with the idea of an appearance in the witness chair, Watkins hesitated. "They make me tell things I don't want to tell," he replied guardedly, his tone sounding more than a little worried. To this forthright statement, said Watkins later, Lincoln's response was spoken with assurance: he "would see to it that he was not questioned about anything but the slung-shot." He didn't say just how he would wall off the witness.

What Watkins' "too much" also involved, what he may or may not have told Lincoln that day in Springfield, was something that when taken with the other evidence would have virtually destroyed Duff's defense. Peering through the moonlight at Walker's Grove, later confessed Watkins, he saw Duff strike Metzger in the face with a weapon ("saw him do it"). But it was not the slung-shot, he thought. It looked like something else, maybe a wagon hammer. All the other defense witnesses saw the same thing, he insisted, some eight or ten of Duff's friends. All testified that Armstrong used only his fists, but "they all swore to a lie and they knew it, as they all knew he hit him with a wagon hammer."

A third element of the defense argument, as Lincoln saw it, concerned the time of night the fight took place, and the related question of how well the scene had been illuminated. Like the Norris lawyers, Lincoln too had checked the almanac for 1857, confirming that at the hour specified there *had* been light enough for anyone to see what happened, of course depending on his distance from the action. Then he noticed something else, a curious discrepancy as to the moon's position.

The prosecution's chief witness, Charles Allen, had placed the moon, at the time of the fight, as having been almost overhead—"about where the sun would be at one o'clock," as he described it. The fight had occurred, as all witnesses agreed, at just about eleven P.M., yet at that hour the almanac placed the moon's position much lower in the sky than "almost overhead," actually down nearer the horizon. Noting the apparent discrepancy, Lincoln was unsure what it indicated, or how it might be used by the defense, if at all. Concerning the amount of illumination shed from the two positions, he knew, there would have been very little difference.

More significantly—and unfortunately, as he admitted—what the almanac really did was bolster the prosecution's claim that the brutal attack on Metzger had been very well lighted, almost as a lurid climactic scene on a theater stage.

As it turned out, Lincoln's whirlwind ten days of preparation for the trial at Beardstown were in a sense wasted. When the case was called on November 19, he was in the courtroom along with no fewer than ten defense witnesses, all arranged a week earlier. Some of them would swear to Duff's good character as a law-abiding citizen, some that he had used nothing in the fight with Metzger but his bare hands, his fists (again, how much coaching the ten may have received from Lincoln cannot now be determined). Unexpectedly, as the proceedings were about to start, the prosecution, led by state's attorney Hugh Fullerton, asked the judge for a continuance. More time, said Fullerton, was needed by the state to make adequate preparation. With the Cass County November term of court nearly finished, that meant putting off the Armstrong case to the spring 1858 term, which would begin May 1. To that request, not an unusual one, the judge readily agreed, Lincoln making no demur.

Fullerton may have been telling at least a partial truth about needing more time to prepare. The real reason, however, as everyone would have recognized, was the involvement of Lincoln in the case, which had become known to the opposition only at the last minute, no doubt a deliberate maneuver. Reasonably enough, Fullerton and his associates had assumed that young Armstrong would be convicted as handily as had his companion in crime. To them the case would have seemed open and shut, needing little more than a replay of the Norris evidence. Lincoln's sudden appearance on the scene swiftly changed all that. It gave warning that some serious complications in the case might be in store, some unpredictable twists and turns. That's why the extra time was needed by the prosecution, getting itself ready to counter any unexpected moves, a well-known Lincoln tactic usually making its entrance "at the critical point of the case."

Lincoln's own personal reaction to the postponement, or the possible reasons for it, is not on record. Certainly, in one way, he must have been pleased and relieved, grateful for the added time to sharpen and refine his presentation, if not to gather still more evidence (the restless Duff, languishing in prison at Beardstown, could not have been too happy about the added months behind bars). Yet in another way he could not have avoided feeling sorely disappointed. Now, for the ensuing six months, a highly critical, indeed pivotal period in his political life, he would have young Armstrong's fate occupying his mind, along with the incessant demands of his regular load of law cases. Then, sometime in May, just as the trial at Beardstown began, the state Republican convention would be looming. Among other things, it would make a final choice of the party's senatorial candidate. Not until then, mid-June, would Lincoln know whether the peculiar threat to his hopes posed by his strange rival, the usurping Democrat Stephen Douglas, would be turned back, leaving the way open for him.

THREE

IN THE COURTROOM

I t was late in the evening when a horse-drawn buggy drew up at the front entrance of the Dunbaugh House on Beardstown's main street. From it stepped Abraham Lincoln, bag in hand and travel-weary. That morning, May 2, 1858, he left Danville on Illinois' eastern border where he'd been practicing in the Vermillion County circuit court. Proceeding by train, in meandering fashion he'd crossed more than half the width of the state to Meredosia, on the Illinois River ten miles below Beardstown, where he hired a buggy and driver. As he entered the Dunbaugh House it was just growing dark.

Before the Armstrong trial was scheduled to come up, five days remained, nearly every hour of which Lincoln planned to spend studying or in consultation with his assistant in the case, the Havana lawyer, William Walker. From his handling of the Norris trial, though he'd lost, Walker possessed an intimate, first-hand knowledge of the fine details of the case, including a familiarity with the witnesses for both sides. To some extent he was also aware how the Havana jury had reacted to the various items of evidence. It was no surprise that Lincoln insisted on asking him to join the defense at Beardstown.

The number of witnesses readied by Lincoln to testify for Duff was double the total he'd summoned back in November. Converging on Beardstown in May were no fewer than twenty-two of Duff's friends, coming from several different counties. Not all were eyewitnesses, about half being there to vouch for Duff's good name. Nelson Watkins, the maker of the slung-shot, was also on hand, still uneasy about taking the stand despite Lincoln's efforts to calm him. Two of Nelson's brothers, George and Jesse Watkins, are also named among the witnesses, perhaps acting more as moral support for their brother than anything else.

Lincoln's intended medical expert, Dr. Charles Parker of Petersburg, would not be subpoenaed until the last moment, the necessary summons being issued the day before the trial. Parker knew well in advance that he'd be called, having already consulted with Lincoln at length. Keeping his name back at first was Lincoln's idea. He didn't want to tip the opposition that he intended making a major issue of the wounds.

The prosecution had also doubled the number of its witnesses from the previous year. In addition to the medical expert, Dr. Stephenson, it called a round dozen men, all but two of them having testified before the grand jury that handed up the original indictment. About half of all the witnesses, defense and prosecution, were like Duff himself illiterate, unable even to sign their names.

By May 5, all the subpoenaed witnesses for both sides had shown up, duly reporting to the court, except one. Charles Allen, whose specific testimony the year before had turned the tide against Norris, had neither signed in nor sent an explanation of his absence. The prosecution had again planned to spotlight the Allen testimony, putting him on the stand as their culminating witness, so another subpoena was issued calling for the sheriff of Menard County to produce Allen "instanter." When the sheriff reported that Allen was nowhere to be found, on the sixth a special writ was issued "to all the sheriffs" of Illinois, commanding them

State of Illinois, } ss.
Cass County,

THE PEOPLE OF THE STATE OF ILLINOIS,
To the Sheriff of ~~Cass~~ *Menard* County GREETING.

We command you to summon *Dr. B. F. Stevenson and Charles Allen*

to be and appear before the Circuit Court of Cass County *Instanter* day of the next Term thereof, ~~to be~~ *now* holden at the Court House in the city of Beardstown _____ _____ in the month of _____ to testify, and the truth to speak in behalf of *the Plaintiffs* in a certain matter of controversy pending in said Court, wherein *the People of the State of Illinois are Plaintiffs* and *William Armstrong* *Defendant*, and have you then and there this writ.

Witness, James Taylor Clerk of said Court, and the Judicial Seal thereof at Beardstown this *5th* day of *May* A. D. 185*8*.

James Taylor CLERK

[Illinoian Print, Beardstown.]

The second summons issued for the pivotal prosecution witness Charles Allen, who had gone into hiding. The doctor named in the same summons (correctly Stephenson) testified for the prosecution at the trial.

to find Allen and bring him in. However, it was not any sheriff who managed to track down the absentee, it was Lincoln himself, whose own trial strategy centered on Allen, also as the concluding witness.

Suspicious about the convenient disappearance, Lincoln questioned Armstrong's brothers, soon wringing from them a reluctant confession. Knowing how crucial would be Allen's testimony, they had foolishly persuaded him to stay away, whether by threats or the promise of money is not known. At that moment the anxious Allen, watched over by two Armstrong cousins, was safely holed up in a little out-of-the-way hotel in the town of Virginia twenty miles away. The disgusted Lincoln, vastly annoyed at this silly and unexpected thwarting by his own side, insisted that the man be brought in immediately. The somewhat surprised Allen on the sixth was fetched from his hiding place, arriving in Beardstown late that evening.

Jury selection moved slowly, as it always does in a murder case, taking at least two days. As expected, a tug of war developed between the prosecution, which wanted older men as being more likely to convict, and the defense, which felt that younger men would be more sympathetic. The result apparently favored the defense, for the average age was under thirty (ages for three members are approximate and for two are not known). Elected as foreman was Milton Logan, of Beardstown, at age thirty-eight among the oldest.

On Monday, May 3, the spring term of the Cass County circuit court began, and four days later, in a courthouse crowded with spectators, the Armstrong case came to trial. Again, state's attorney Hugh Fullerton led the prosecution, now assisted by Henry Shaw, a Beardstown lawyer well known to Lincoln (the two had several times joined forces in previous Cass County cases). Occupying most of the seats behind the defendant's table were the Armstrongs, Hannah with her sons, flanked by a large contingent of relatives and friends. Back of the prosecutor's table sat Metzger's family and friends, including his wife. On the bench was James Harriott, judge of the Twenty-first Judicial Circuit, aged forty-eight, the same man who had presided at the Norris trial.

Always a notable presence in a courtroom because of his unusual height and his striking, clean-shaven features with their strong, angular planes, on this morning Lincoln attracted even more attention. Instead of his customary dark suit, he was dressed entirely in white, making him stand out dramatically from the uniform blacks, browns, and dull grays worn by all the other men. This could not have been the only time in his life that Lincoln wore a white suit, yet, curiously, it is the only time that the fact was recorded. After the trial that day a Beardstown photographer asked him to pose and the picture still exists.

Also sitting close behind the defense table was a young lawyer just beginning in practice named Abram Bergen (later a respected judge in the area). Having watched and been fascinated by Lincoln in several previous trials, he wanted to see how Springfield's leading lawyer handled a murder indictment—"how a good lawyer examined witnesses," as he said, "and the manner of doing work in a court in detail not found in books." In the short interval before the trial commenced, with all the participants sitting and waiting patiently, Bergen studied the rugged face of the defense counsel at an angle and was powerfully struck by "the irregularity of the profile," and by the way the shaggy brow dominated the whole face:

. . . the lowest part of his forehead projected beyond his eyes to a greater degree than any other person's that I have ever seen. From the front, his eyes looked very deep-set and sunken, by reason of this abnormal extension of the frontal bone. He sat among the lawyers . . . with his head thrown back, his steady gaze apparently fixed on one spot of the blank ceiling, without the least change in the direction of his dull, expressionless eyes, without noticing anything transpiring around him, and without any variation of feature, or

movement of any muscle of his face. I suppose he was thinking of the coming case.

At that moment the silent Lincoln was indeed thinking of the
coming case, but in ways that neither Bergen nor anyone else who
knew him, knew his deserved reputation as a lawyer for fair and
upright dealing, could ever have guessed. The impassiveness noted
by the perceptive Bergen that morning actually revealed Lincoln in
a quietly desperate mood, ready to do violence to the principals
that had always guided him. His sensitive spirit stirred to its
utmost by that old debt of gratitude, he was preparing to subvert
the law, something he'd never been known to do before, and
apparently never did again.

At the invitation of Judge Harriott, state's attorney Fullerton
rose to begin the prosecution's case. Carefully he explained to the
attentive jury all that he intended to prove, then he proceeded to
call a parade of witnesses to the chair, ten young men who'd seen
the fight. Rapidly, in more or less detail, each described what he
remembered of the ugly scene, how the powerful Metzger had
been set upon by the two smaller men, Armstrong wielding the
wicked slung-shot. That phase of the state's case went speedily,
taking probably less than two hours.

Next came Dr. Stephenson to discuss the skull wounds, and tell
precisely how, separately or together, they had been the direct if
delayed cause of death. It was still short of noontime when Charles
Allen took the stand.

By now well rehearsed, Allen's graphic testimony was spun out
in deliberate fashion. His personal acquaintance with Armstrong,
his distance from the combatants, the position of the moon and its
degree of brightness, the cloud-free night sky—all were minutely
covered. Fullerton also had the witness stand up and, using
another man to represent Metzger, demonstrate the manner in
which the accused had delivered the blow, about at the level of
Metzger's forehead, hitting the brow-ridge and in toward the nose.

Swinging the actual weapon in the little demonstration would have been too dangerous. Instead, as Allen lifted his arm to show the angle, Fullerton held the slung-shot high for the jury's inspection, the small, leather-covered weight dangling menacingly at the end of a stout, foot-long cord.

There came a break for lunch, after which the defense took the floor. Going back into the courtroom, Lincoln pulled the worried Hannah aside. His own presentation, he said, would require about the same amount of time as had the prosecution. Depending on the length of the jury's deliberations, the trial should be over that very day. If so, he added confidently, her boy would "be cleared before sun down."

Lincoln too began by anticipating for the jury what he was, as he said, about to prove—that young Armstrong was innocent of all charges, including the lesser one of manslaughter that had been sustained against Norris. This would become plain from two simple facts. First, Armstrong had used *no* weapon in the fight, nothing but his fists. Second, the frontal fracture to Metzger's skull was an unfortunate but undeniable result of the occipital fracture, the wound to the *back* of the head caused by the other man, already convicted for the crime. Nor had Armstrong acted in concert with that other man, whose fatal assault on Metzger had taken place some minutes *before* Armstrong's fist-fight with the victim.

The unlucky Duff, stressed Lincoln, was guilty only of losing his temper, and even then he'd been sorely provoked. Which of the jurymen would laugh it off if he was violently dumped flat on the ground while asleep? Armstrong, weighing barely 140 pounds and standing five foot four, should rather be admired for taking on an opponent a great deal bigger, heavier, and stronger than himself. Was young Duff to be blamed because another small man on being similarly insulted by the drunken Metzger had sought revenge with a club?

The first witnesses put on by Lincoln readily admitted Duff's occasional rowdy behavior, in taverns and at the horse racing he loved—hardly different from lots of other young bucks, children of the hardy pioneers who'd carved Illinois out of the wilderness. But all insisted on his unblemished character as a man among his friends and before the law. Never once had he been charged with any sort of infraction, a worthy son of his widowed mother (did Lincoln here turn and indicate the presence of the bonneted, sorrowful-looking Hannah?).

Next in a steady parade came the eyewitnesses, probably a dozen or more. Answering Lincoln's questions, each stated just where he'd been standing that night, how far he was from the action, and ended by swearing that Duff's hands had been empty. The few punches he'd succeeded in landing on the taller Metzger had all been delivered by a closed fist, producing little effect on their bulky target. As to the slung-shot, none of these witnesses admitted to having seen or heard of such a weapon at the campgrounds that night. Lincoln also queried each witness as to the hour the fight took place. A few couldn't be sure but from most came the same assured reply: it had been at or about eleven o'clock.

Next to the stand came Nelson Watkins, and Lincoln's nerves must have tightened just a bit. As Watkins settled uneasily in the raised witness chair, Lincoln held up the slung-shot. Did Watkins recognize it?

Yes, he answered. It belonged to him. He'd made it himself, at home.

What was inside the leather casing?

A metal ball.

What sort of metal?

Copper, with a thin lead skin.

Where had Watkins gotten hold of an unusual chunk of metal like that?

Cast it himself, copper and lead.

Lincoln took a knife, cut a slit in the leather, and extracted the rough metal ball. On the dull lead surface he made a few quick scratches exposing the reddish copper. Then he passed the ball to the jury. Each of the twelve examined it closely, rubbing and chafing with a finger.

Lincoln continued: Did Watkins bring the slung-shot with him to Walker's Grove on the night of August 29?

Yes he did.

That night, did he lend it to anyone?

No he didn't.

Did the accused, Duff Armstrong, ever at any time that night have the weapon in his possession?

No.

The weapon had been found several days later near the scene of the crime. How could Watkins explain that?

A little nervously, Watkins gave the story as he'd told it to Lincoln in the office: he fell asleep under a wagon and on waking forgot that he'd left the slung-shot on the wagon frame. He supposed it was carried away when the wagon departed next morning, and at some point had dropped off.

Was he positive that after his sleep under the wagon he didn't see the weapon again that night, in fact not until that very moment there in the court?

Yes, he was positive.

Thank you, said Lincoln, and the witness was dismissed.

Whether any of the jury noticed the look of relief on Watkins' face as he stepped down from the witness chair can't be said. If anyone did catch it, certainly its real significance wasn't guessed. More pertinent is the question of Fullerton's response, how the prosecution reacted to such a wrenching of what had seemed established fact. The strange thing is that nowhere in the existing record, primary or secondary, is there the least hint that Fullerton did anything at all about the Watkins assertions. How Lincoln managed it remains a mystery, but his promise that Watkins wouldn't be harried or pressed by the prosecution seems to have been fulfilled.

Still, it is hard to think that Fullerton would have let Watkins depart in complete silence. Though the record fails to show it, perhaps he did retain the witness at least long enough to ask about Duff's possible *use* of the weapon, no matter who made or owned it. Of course the simple tale about the slung-shot having rested out of sight beneath the wagon would not have been easily called into question. At best, the prosecuting attorney might have been able to indicate a bare possibility that Duff, unknown to Watkins, had in some accidental way come across the weapon, under the wagon or elsewhere. The focus of the questioning then—if Fullerton was sharp enough to spot the opening—would have shifted to such things as the length of Watkins' nap and the precise time he awakened, threatening sensitive areas Lincoln had vowed to avoid. But for whatever reason nothing came of it, and Watkins's crucial testimony passed virtually unchallenged.

The next witness called was Dr. Parker, and as he approached the stand everyone could see that he was carrying a human skull. In his questioning of the physician Lincoln proceeded to display a fairly precise knowledge of cranial anatomy, so much so that it surprised his opponents as well as other legal minds in the courtroom including young Bergen. Keeping the skull visible to the jury, he discussed its various parts and their relation to each other, sounding almost as if he were a surgeon about to operate.

Could striking one spot on the human cranium and inflicting an injury, asked Lincoln, cause a similar injury to another part, say on the side opposite?

Yes, of course, replied Parker. Multiple injuries from a single blow could happen to any rigid structure.

Would a fracture here (a finger points at the center of the skull's rear) possibly result in a break here (the skull is turned and a finger traces a line down the lower forehead to the corner of the right eye socket).

Depending on the force and direction of the blow, yes, it could easily cause two such fractures.

The picture that emerged from this exchange, of both breaks being produced by a single terrible blow, was utterly convincing to many of the listeners (afterwards Judge Harriott said that the Parker testimony was the defense's single most important piece of evidence). For good measure, Lincoln then led Dr. Parker to comment on the admitted fact that Metzger, going home, had fallen at least twice off his moving mount. Readily, Parker agreed that falling from the height of a horse's back, if the head struck the ground, could have produced the frontal fracture, certainly would have seriously aggravated an existing wound.

By now, many in the courtroom, including Fullerton and his co-counsel, Henry Shaw, were starting to feel that Duff's chances for winning an acquittal were fast improving, getting better by the minute. Standing now between him and freedom, it appeared, was only one man, the prosecution's pivotal witness, Charles Allen. A calm, assured personality, a man of some education in contrast to most of his friends, his detailed description of what he claimed to have seen, a description exact and specific, had been compelling. When Lincoln called him back to the stand for cross-examination a murmur rippled through the crowd.

Two incisive observations made later by one of the jurymen, John Brady, set the scene for what happened next, how the friendly questioner controlled the unwary Allen, leading him deftly on toward the climactic instant. The first observation shows Lincoln exacting from Allen a firm commitment as to the moon's *position*, its being nearly overhead: "Mr. Lincoln was very particular to have him repeat himself a dozen times or more during the trial about where the moon was located." The second shows that Lincoln was not at all backward about putting words in Allen's mouth, actually, it would seem, successfully coaching or leading a hostile witness! "Mr. Lincoln was very careful," reported Brady, "not to cross Mr. Allen in anything, and when Allen lacked words to express himself, Lincoln loaned them to him." Brady, it is certain, was paying strict attention to the little drama unfolding a few feet away from him, especially the demeanor and technique of the white-suited defense counsel. It's likely that the other eleven men were equally captivated.

His tone relaxed, Lincoln's opening questions would have been simple ones. Where did Allen live? Was he a frequent visitor to Walker's Grove? On the night in question what time did he arrive at the grove? Had he seen Duff that night before the fight, talked to him? Had he himself been drinking? Allen's answers were equally relaxed. Yes, like all the others he did take some whiskey, but unlike the others he wasn't drunk.

From there Lincoln quickly narrowed his aim to his real target, the moon (the ensuing exchange while not detailed in the court records is easily recovered from the surviving evidence).

How far from the fight had Allen been standing?

Twenty yards, maybe.

Say fifty or sixty feet? No more?

About that.

The fight took place, you say, at just about eleven P.M., an hour before midnight. At sixty feet no doubt you could see the figures of the struggling men all right. But even with the moon shining you couldn't really be sure what they were holding in their hands, could you?

It was a bright moon, three-quarters moon. I could see everything, everybody.

Here Lincoln asked the witness to stand up and demonstrate how the blow of the slung-shot was delivered. Allen "got up and went through the motion, struck an overhand blow," which Lincoln asked him to repeat. Confidently he again lifted his arm, swinging it up and over.

Was the accused *facing* Metzger when he hit him, asked Lincoln.

Yes.

Directly in front of him or off to the side?

In front.

You're sure that the weapon was held in the right hand of the accused?

Yes.

The blow was delivered from over the shoulder, not from the side or from below?

Yes.

Asking the witness to resume his seat, Lincoln went on. You were able to see all this physical detail at a distance of fifty or sixty feet and at eleven o'clock at night because the whole scene was brightly lit by the moon?

Yes.

A three-quarters moon.

Yes.

From where you were standing watching the fight, where was the moon? Up behind you? Over your shoulder? In front? Off to the side?

Up high. About overhead.

Not exactly overhead?

A little past overhead. Down a little.

But nearly overhead.

Yes.

And it was very bright?

Yes. Bright.

In that vicinity there are a lot of trees, and the lay of the land slopes down some, into a sort of wide depression. Isn't it true that the moon's light was interrupted, cut off? It didn't shine directly down on the scene now, did it?

Yes it did. It was high up. Shone right down, nothing in the way. No trees.

Please describe the moon's position more exactly. What does the phrase *high up* mean in precise terms?

Means about where the sun is at, say, one o'clock in the daytime. A little past overhead.

To see it, look up at it, you'd have to bend your head back a little I suppose?

Yes.

And it was bright, shining right down on the fighters?

I told you it was.

You could recognize their faces even from sixty feet?

Sure I could. Easy.

I ask you again whether you are positive about the moon's *position* that night, its *size* and its *strength*. Wasn't it really much dimmer than you claim? Much lower in the sky? Wasn't it too dim for you to be sure of *anything* at sixty feet?

I told you it was a *bright* moon. High up! Above my head, almost. Not full, but bright.

Turning, Lincoln walked slowly back to the defense table, and opened a briefcase. From it he drew three small, thin, paper covered booklets. One he handed to Fullerton at the other table, then he walked to the bench where he handed another up to the judge. It was a *Jayne's Almanac* from the previous year, 1857, he explained, a copy of which he held in his hand. Would the judge please open to the page for August?

Turning to Allen, he asked if he was still certain about the moon's size, strength, and especially its position at eleven o'clock on the night in question, August 29, 1857?

Yes, he was still sure (said with perhaps a tinge of uncertainty as Allen gazed at the pamphlet in Lincoln's hand).

Did Allen understand the term *moonset*? Did he know that it referred to the moon's *upper edge* disappearing below the horizon?

I guess.

Well, said Lincoln, that is the technical meaning of the term as used by astronomers. At moonset the entire moon is gone, sinking below the horizon. Holding the little booklet high he waved it gently back and forth.

Mr. Allen, this is an almanac for the year 1857. It gives the exact time of moonset for every day of the year in central Illinois.

Looking at the page for August, and tracing down the column about the moon, we see that on the twenty-ninth, the night of the fight, moonset came at *three minutes after midnight*. In other words, at eleven o'clock—only one short hour before moonset— the moon was nowhere near overhead. It was *way* down. In fact it was sitting about smack on the horizon, getting itself ready to disappear from sight!

From among the spectators burst a "roar of laughter," even from many of the jurors, the hilarity rising steadily. Irritably, Judge Harriott gaveled it down. Then he bent and peered closely at the little volume in his hand.

Leaving the stricken Allen—to the jury, as several of them said later, he looked as if he'd been "floored"—Lincoln handed the almanac to the jury foreman, Milton Logan. After a minute's inspection, Logan passed it to the next man, and it went along from juror to juror until all twelve had taken a look. In the court, except for a low buzzing among the spectators, silence reigned.

After a few moments, Fullerton called a clerk over and sent him downstairs in the courthouse to see if he could locate another 1857 almanac, one issued by a different publisher. The man soon returned and handed the prosecutor two almanacs, one of them a *Goudy's*, the other an *Ayer's*. Together, Fullerton and his assistant Shaw compared them with the almanac supplied by Lincoln and found that all three agreed as to the hour of moonset the night of the killing. (The *Ayer's*, calculated for a slightly higher latitude than the *Jayne's*—New York City rather than Philadelphia—was ahead of the *Jayne's* by two minutes, of course not a significant difference for Lincoln's argument. The *Goudy's* would have been about the same, showing a difference of only a few minutes even if calculated for the latitude of Boston.)

Saying not another word, Lincoln sat down. So far as he could tell at that moment, his gamble had paid off. He'd taken an undoubted fact, one that fully supported the *prosecution's* case— that the moon had not set, had in fact been a whole hour from set-

Cover of an 1857 Jayne's Almanac, a copy of the one introduced by Lincoln at the trial. Other almanacs have been proposed as the one used but the jury foreman is on record as insisting that it was a Jayne's.

The Eighth Month, or AUGUST, 1857.

[illegible] for the Latitudes of the New England States, Canada, New York, New Jersey, Pennsylvania, Delaware, Maryland, North Virginia, Ohio, Indiana, Illinois, Michigan, Wisconsin, Iowa, North Missouri, and North California.

		Lat. of Boston. Sun rises h. m.	Sun sets h. m.	Moon Rises h. m.	Sun slow	Lat. of Philada. Sun rises h. m.	Sun sets h. m.	Moon Rises h. m.	Moon's Signs s.	d.	Moon south h. m.	Aspects of Planets and other Miscellanies.	Old St.
1	S.	4 51	7 9	0 21	6	4 57	7 3	0 32		22	8 59	Antares s. 7 h. 38 m.	20
(31)	8th Sunday after Trinity.						Matt. 7.					Day's Length 14 h. 6 min.	
2	S.	4 52	7 8	1 8	6	4 58	7 2	1 20		4	9 54	Lyra s. 9 h. 45 m.	21
3	M.	4 53	7 7	2 6	6	4 59	7 1	2 17		17	10 48	♀ rises 1 h. 45 m.	22
4	T.	4 55	7 5	3 12	6	5 0	7 0	3 22		0	11 42	Altair s. 10 h. 49 m.	23
5	W.	4 56	7 4	Rises.	6	5 1	6 59	Rises.		13	morn.	5th.	24
6	T.	4 57	7 3	8 0	6	5 2	6 58	7 57		26	0 33	Fomal. s. 1h. 50m.	25
7	F.	4 58	7 2	8 24	5	5 [illegible]	6 57	8 23		10	1 21	♃ □ ☉	26
8	S.	4 59	7 1	8 44	5	5 4	6 56	8 45		23	2 9	♄ rises 8 h. 34 m.	27
(32)	9th Sunday after Trinity.						Luke 16.					Day's Length 13 h. 50 min.	
9	S.	5 0	7 0	9 6	5	5 5	6 55	9 9		7	2 55	Arietes s. 4 h. 47 m.	28
10	M.	5 1	6 59	9 30	5	5 6	6 54	9 35		21	3 42		29
11	T.	5 3	6 58	9 56	5	5 7	6 53	10 3		5	4 32	Algenib s. 2 h. 47 m.	30
12	W.	5 4	6 56	10 29	5	5 9	6 51	10 38		19	5 24	12th. ☽ in Perig.	31
13	T.	5 5	6 55	11 10	5	5 10	6 50	11 22		4	6 21	♅ ☌ ☽	1
14	F.	5 6	6 54	morn.	4	5 11	6 49	morn.		18	7 21	♃ south 5 h. 18 m.	2
15	S.	5 7	6 53	0 8	4	5 12	6 48	0 16		2	8 24	Markab s. 1 h. 23 m.	3
(33)	10th Sunday after Trinity.						Luke 19.					Day's Length 13 h. 34 min.	
16	S.	5 9	6 42	1 7	4	5 13	6 47	1 19		16	9 26	♀ ☌ ☽ ♄ ☌ ☽	4
17	M.	5 10	6 41	2 20	4	5 14	6 46	2 31		0	10 25	Lyra s. 8 h. 47 m.	5
18	T.	5 11	6 40	Sets.	4	5 15	6 45	Sets.		14	11 19	Altair s. 9 h. 54 m.	6
19	W.	5 13	6 38	7 11	3	5 16	6 43	7 8		27	12 9	19th. ☿ in ☋	7
20	T.	5 14	6 37	7 32	3	5 18	6 42	7 31		10	12 54	Fomal. s. 1 h. 0 m.	8
21	F.	5 15	6 36	7 52	3	5 19	6 41	7 53		23	1 37	☿ ☌ ☽	9
22	S.	5 17	6 34	8 10	3	5 20	6 40	8 12		6	2 18	♅ □ ☉	10
(34)	11th Sunday after Trinity.						Luke 18.					Day's Length 13 h. 18 min.	
23	S.	5 18	6 51	8 28	2	5 21	6 39	8 32		18	2 59	Markab s. 0 h. 50 m.	11
24	M.	5 19	6 50	8 47	2	5 22	6 38	8 53		0	3 40	♄ rises 2 h. 14 m.	12
25	T.	5 20	6 49	9 12	2	5 24	6 36	9 20		12	4 23	Altair s. 9 h. 30 m.	13
26	W.	5 22	6 47	9 40	2	5 25	6 35	9 50		24	5 9	☽ in Apogee.	14
27	T.	5 23	6 46	10 14	1	5 26	6 34	10 25		6	5 57	27th.	15
28	F.	5 24	6 45	10 58	1	5 27	6 33	11 10		18	6 49	Algenib s. 1 h. 40 m.	16
29	S.	5 26	6 43	11 51	1	5 29	6 31	morn.		0	7 42	♀ ☌ ♄; ☿ in Aphelion.	17
(35)	12th Sunday after Trinity.						Mark 7.					Day's Length 13 h. 0 min.	
30	S.	5 27	6 33	morn.	0	5 30	6 30	0 3		12	8 36	Fomalhaut s. 0 h. 16 m.	18
31	M	5 29	6 31	0 53	0	5 31	6 29	1 5		25	9 30	Arietes s. 3 h. 20 m.	19

Moon's Phases.

	Philadelphia. dy. h. m.	Boston. dy. h. m.
Full Moon,	5, 1 28.1 A.	5, 1 44.5 A.
Last Quarter,	12, 12 41.5 A.	12, 12 57.9 A.
New Moon,	19, 11 25.7 M.	19, 11 42.1 M.
First Quarter,	27, 10 3.8 M.	27, 10 20.2 M.

Conjectures of the Weather!

The 1st—3d clear, very pleasant; 4th, 5th changeable; 6th, 7th pleasant; 8th—10th cloudy, rain; 11th thunder; 12th, 13th cloudy; 14th—16th mostly clear; 17th—19th pleasant; 20th cloudy; 21st—23d dry, clear; 24th, 25th thunder; 26th, 27th cloudy, rainy; 28th—31st clear.

DECLINE!

J. H. Normeny, Esq., Postmaster, Berkley, Ala., writes: July 11th, 1851.

During the last year, Mr. Morgan Gibson, of Madison Co., Ala., applied for the Expectorant and Sanative Pills under the following circumstances—he had been for some time previous in a decline, was greatly emaciated, and with such entire prostration of his system, that the attending physicians very candidly told him their services could no longer avail him any thing—medicine was useless, and the administration of any more in his case would but prolong his sufferings and agony! A friend, however, had advised him to try Dr. Jayne's Medicines; he procured a few bottles

23

[To be continued, see month of September.]

Page for August from Jayne's Almanac, *used by Lincoln to obscure the testimony of Charles Allen. Moonset for the 29th occurred just after twelve at night so the actual time for moonset is listed as of the morning of the 30th, in the almanac expressed as 0:03.*

ting, thus giving ample light for Allen and the other eyewitnesses to see by—and had deftly clouded the jury's perception of that fact, so that it appeared to support the *defense*. Whether the mistaken perception would hold its place in the jury's mind long enough to supply a cap to the already strong presentation, he could only hope.

No alert prosecutor could possibly allow a defense attorney to get away with such a slickly distorting maneuver. Fullerton's response to the clever ploy would have been to detain Allen in the witness chair, asking him to state again whether, aside from the question of the moon's exact position, there had been enough light to see by. To this, Allen naturally would have responded that yes, there had definitely been more than enough light. No doubt Fullerton also fed Allen questions designed to soften his error about the moon being high rather than low. Allen's answer is obvious: he hadn't taken particular notice of the moon's position at the time—who would?—and then in looking back assumed that it had been high because it was so bright. Now it was Fullerton's turn to wonder how well Allen's rebuttal would take with the attentive jury.

The witnessing of an event by moonlight can be a very difficult situation to judge with accuracy after the fact, so it is at least curious that no historian of the Armstrong case bothered to investigate what seeing by moonlight is really like. On that score—and because it helps recapture some of the courtroom discussion of the topic now lost—a brief interruption of the narrative to describe a few simple experiments made by this author seems warranted.

On a dozen nights in cold weather and mild I stood in an open field under cloudless, moonlit skies gauging what detail could be discerned in what degree of illumination at what distances. On each occasion I placed myself at varying positions in relation to different targets (such as a tree on whose boughs I'd hung several objects, or bulkier things like barrels and different colored buckets set on chairs). Soon enough I was struck by a fact I should have anticipated: the results were never twice the same. Though a casual eye might see conditions as very similar, a slight alteration in any one element brought a noticeable change in visibility.

Simply specifying that the moon was in a certain phase or was at a particular elevation would never be enough to capture the reality of one specific night's setting.

Where detail is concerned, everything depends on a shifting combination of elements: the exact strength and placement of the moon, the precise degree of darkness otherwise, the observer's angle of vision and distance from the object, the size and coloring of the object itself. No mere description attempted afterward, no citing of technical data alone, can hope to delineate a particular scene in all its subtle shades and qualities. Only a witness who was actually present on a designated night, who retains the feel and memory of the particular fleeting combination of factors, can tell what was or was not see-able.

One measurement of significance did show up, not surprisingly related to distance. Ten or fifteen yards—forty or perhaps fifty feet—really seems to be the farthest at which an observer can be at all sure of detail, even on what would be considered an especially bright night. Moonlight is never at any time what may be called vivid, is never really bright (it's that only by comparison). Always fuzzy or hazy, it lacks the pure, penetrating clarity of the sun or electric light. *Spectral* is a term much favored by writers to limn the peculiar effect of moonlight.

If Charles Allen had been standing as far from the crime scene as 150 feet, the distance often specified in prior accounts of the case, he would never have thought of claiming certainty about what he saw. He and the others on both sides of the question would have been well aware of all these limiting factors. Even then

I suspect that there was a bit more to it, and that Allen—whether or not the fact came up in court—knew beforehand what kind of weapon Duff was carrying. Watching the fight, he recognized the deadly slung-shot in Duff's hand as it delivered that sweeping overhand blow to Metzger's face.

Especially liable to misjudgment is the gauging of the moon's height or position when done with relation to fixed objects in the immediate vicinity (buildings, trees, hills). A watcher need only move to a different spot to alter his perception drastically. When a line of sight includes a nearby object and a far distant one, the location of the distant object is promptly and radically changed by a movement of only a few paces. If the move transfers the moon to a wide expanse of clear sky, the *elevation* in particular can deceptively appear to be quite altered. That fact alone could go far in explaining Charles Allen's error on the witness stand as to the moon's height.

In one of my experiments I placed the moon just above a house chimney and beside the bulky shadow of a tall, spreading tree. I then walked back and off to the side, a distance of no more than twenty feet. Immediately on looking up again I saw that the moon—now shining in solitary splendor in an unimpeded sweep of sky—actually appeared to be much higher and considerably brighter than it had a moment before. It was, I might add, a waxing, three-quarters moon, the same as shone on central Illinois the night of the fight in 1857.

It was late afternoon in the crowded Beardstown courtroom when the presentation of evidence finally ended and closing arguments were called for, prosecutor Fullerton's coming first. An able summation, it stressed the eyewitness testimony that had proved so effective in convicting Norris. Fullerton also described several ways, fairly obvious, in which Armstrong could have come into possession of the slung-shot. Dr. Parker's opinion about the wounds he challenged by citing his own expert witness's disagreement (on exactly what anatomical basis is not now discoverable). Insisting that Armstrong and Norris had attacked in concert, he also declared that the scene *had* been well lighted. The very almanac introduced by the defense *proved* the fact. That the moon was low at the critical moment didn't mean anything. A three-quarters moon in an unclouded sky a full hour from setting would have given plenty of light!

When Fullerton had done talking, neither he nor anyone else in the courtroom could be sure of the effect on the jury.

What happened next, the defense summation by Lincoln, long since has taken a special place in the inspiring tale of his life, as well as in the colorful annals of courtroom drama. His passionate plea to the jury, in which he risked adding a personal factor to the argument, has become a classic of emotional persuasion. Here again, however, the legend is rather different from the truth—considerably different, it should be said. The more accurate version, for some, will even stand as far more interesting than the myth because making infinitely more sense.

In his character as a public speaker, in court or at political meetings, Lincoln was not the quiescent, somber-voiced figure so often portrayed in films. His delivery was animated, yet with an instinctive self-control in which a note of underplaying left an impression of naturalness. His law partner, William Herndon, who heard him speak hundreds of times, on large occasions and small, in court and out, provides the best description ever penned of Lincoln before an audience. It is an offhand sketch couched in Herndon's own effective if nervous style, all the more graphic for being unstudied:

When he rose to speak to the jury or to crowds of people, he stood inclined forward, was awkward, ungainly, odd, and, being a very sensitive man, I think that it added to his awkwardness . . . [his] voice was, when he first began speaking, shrill, squeaking, piping, unpleasant; his general look, his form, his pose, the color of his flesh, wrinkled and dry, his sensitiveness and momentary diffidence, everything seemed to be against him, but he soon recovered.

I can see him now, in my mind distinct. On rising to address the jury or the crowd he quite generally placed his hands behind him . . . as he proceeded he moved his hands to the front of his person, generally interlocking his fingers and running one thumb around the other . . . growing warmer he used his hands—especially his right hand—in his gestures.

He used his head a great deal, throwing or jerking or moving it now here now there, now in this position and now in that, in order to be more emphatic, to drive the idea home . . . [he] did not gesticulate much, and yet it is true that every organ of his body was in motion . . . gradually he warmed up; his shrill, squeaking voice became harmonious, melodious, musical if you please, with face somewhat aglow.

In addressing the Armstrong jury, it is said, the utter sincerity of Lincoln's moving, even tearful description of the Armstrong family's goodness to him in his youth brought answering tears from the stolid jurymen, melting their crusted hearts. "The last 15 minutes of his speech," recalled co-counsel Walker, "were as eloquent as I ever heard, and such the power & earnestness with which he spoke, that jury & all sat as if entranced, & when he was through found relief in a gush of tears. I have never seen such mastery exhibited over the feelings and emotions of men as on that occasion."

Others who were present in the court that day agreed, more or less, with that estimate. What no one seems to have suspected is that the earnestness and the sincerity, so obvious to all, were by no means unalloyed, but were as much a part of the carefully planned defense as the questioning of the hostile witnesses. In his summation, as in every smallest facet of the case, Lincoln left nothing to chance. The closing histrionics were all well calculated, and display a side of Lincoln's personality and practice seldom noticed.

In an earlier case where he represented the widow of a Revolutionary War soldier, his notes for the summation still survive. They help make real what happened in Beardstown: "No contract. Not professional services. Unreasonable charge . . . Revolutionary War. Describe Valley Forge privations. Ice. Soldier's bleeding feet. Plaintiff's husband. Soldier leaving home for army. *Skin defendant.* Close." On that occasion the summation went as planned, and when he had done tying in the aged, crippled widow with her husband's hardships in the war, the jury were so moved that "half of them were in tears." Lincoln always knew just when and if it would pay to wring tears from a jury, and was supremely confident he could do it when needed. He'd already decided it would be needed at Beardstown.

A case he'd handled four years previously catches him in a very similar instance of courtroom dramatics, a performance preserved in some detail by an eyewitness. It so much resembles, from a slightly different angle, what is reported of his actions at Beardstown—where little of the detail was saved—that the passage should be read whole. In that earlier case he was defending a Colonel Dunlap, who was being sued for damages by the victim in a public assault:

> It came Lincoln's turn to speak. He dragged his huge feet off the table on the top of which they had been calmly resting, set them on the floor; gradually lifted up and partly straightened out his great length of legs and body, and took off his coat. While he was removing his coat, I and all the others noticed his eyes very intently fixed on something on the table before him.

He picked up the object, a paper, from the table. Scrutinizing it closely and without having uttered a word, he broke out into a long, loud, peculiar laugh, accompanied by his most wonderfully funny facial expression . . . The whole audience grinned. He laid the paper down, slowly took off his cravat; again picked up the paper, looked at it again, and repeated the laugh. It was contagious. By that time all in the packed courtroom were tittering . . .

He then took off his vest, showing his one yarn suspender, took up the paper, again looked at it and again indulged in his own loud peculiar laugh. Its effect was absolutely irresistible. The usually solemn and dignified Judge Woodson, the Jury, and the whole audience could hold themselves no longer, and broke out into a long, loud continued roar; all this before Lincoln had uttered a word. I call this acting . . .

He apologized to the court for his seemingly rude behavior and explained that the damages as claimed were at first written as $1000. He supposed that the plaintiff afterwards had taken a second look at the colonel's pile, and had thereupon concluded that the wounds to his honor were worth $10,000.

The result of this performance, as planned, was to destroy any chance the plaintiff had for coming away with a penny more than the original thousand dollars. Apparently none of the jurors paused long enough to wonder why Lincoln hadn't earlier noticed the change in the sum, why it hadn't struck him until that day in court. If any had, the little trick might have backfired. But Lincoln took the risk.

At Beardstown, the casual disrobing act, again with emphasis on the yarn suspenders, also preceded any words, a fact vividly recalled by one of the jurors, John Brady. As the white-suited Lincoln approached the jury box, "he removed his coat, vest, and later, his stock, the old-fashioned necktie . . . his suspenders were

Travel and attendance vouchers for two important witnesses at the Armstrong trial, Charles Allen and Nelson Watkins. The mileages specified are the distances between the men's homes and Beardstown doubled.

home-made knitted ones, and finally as he warmed up to his subject one of them slipped from his shoulder, and he let it fall to his
side where it remained until he had finished speaking." According
to Brady, who didn't for a moment suspect Lincoln of putting on
an act, all this, the drooping suspenders in particular, gave Lincoln's closing speech a down-home, "backwoodsy" feel, smacking
of the honest old "prairie lawyer" image. (This particular prairie
lawyer only weeks before had received the then enormous fee of
$5,000 from the Illinois Central Railroad for winning a very intri-
cate case of tax liability. So unusually large was the payment asked
by Lincoln that the railroad balked at paying it and Lincoln had to
sue his own clients to collect.)

The talk that followed, said Brady, was full of "fiery eloquence . . . masterly argument," finishing up with a moving passage of "tender and pathetic pleading for the life of the son of his
old benefactors." The arresting fact that Brady, as he admitted
years afterward, *believed* the damning testimony of Charles Allen
against Duff, yet *still* voted not guilty, is perhaps the best commen-
tary on Lincoln's view both of how the defense should go, and his
striking ability in summing up.

However, as with almost every detail of the trial, the prevailing
legend about that eloquent closing speech simply gets it wrong,
almost precisely opposite to the reality. It wasn't one lengthy,
heartwringing cry that had Lincoln begging for the life of the
young defendant. The time occupied by the talk was well under an
hour, for most of which Lincoln, coldly analytical, rehearsed the
evidence minutely, with emphasis on the testimony of Watkins
and Dr. Parker.

Concerning Charles Allen and the moon, he trod very carefully
indeed. Not wishing to dilute the crushing effect produced by the
almanac, wary of allowing the jurors time to rethink the moment,
he merely pointed out the obvious: if Allen was so badly mistaken
about where the brightly shining moon had been, then he was
very probably mistaken about the other things he'd sworn to

(onlookers could almost see some of the jurymen nodding in silent agreement).

Only as he came to the end did Lincoln switch gears, sliding subtly from a coldly legal mood into the personal. "He told of his kind feelings," recalled Walker, "toward the mother of the prisoner, a widow, that she had been kind to him when *he* was young, lone, & without friends." Opposing counsel Henry Shaw, in a letter written only eight years after the trial, sketched some of the detail of what Lincoln actually said about the help he'd received as a young man from the Armstrongs:

> He told the jury of his once being a poor, friendless boy; that Armstrong's father took him into his house, fed & clothed him & gave him a home etc., the particulars of which were told so pathetically that the jury forgot the guilt of the boy in their admiration of the father. It was generally admitted that Lincoln's speech and personal appeal to the jury saved Armstrong.

Here was calculation indeed, in the form of quite deliberate exaggeration—to put it plainly, Lincoln was telling a whopper. The amiable Jack "took him into his house" all right, but only now and then, whenever Lincoln felt like visiting. Back in New Salem he had his own regular living arrangements. "Fed him," yes, but on occasion only, and it could hardly be said that the Armstrongs "clothed him," unless he meant those times when Hannah sewed a rip in his trousers or made him a shirt or did some of his wash. *Gave him a home?* Not exactly, not in the absolute sense in which the jurors would have understood the phrase.

Yet there's another, equally pertinent fact to be noted: as Lincoln talked to the jury something happened inside him, wholly unexpected—a spark was lit. Underlying all his lawyerly calculations there lay the deeper truth of his genuine and profoundly felt debt to Jack Armstrong, creator of the "turning point" in his aimless young life. It was that pressing if momentarily submerged emotion, made infinitely more urgent by Jack's dying request, that welled suddenly up, whirling him far past his intended role of mere pleader.

Now as he talked he was carried back through twenty years, and in his mind's eye he again vividly saw the humble old Armstrong cabin with Hannah at the fire surrounded by her children. Again he heard the roar of the partisan crowd as he struggled in the ring with his powerful opponent, felt the heat, felt the dust rising. As he spoke, his clear, tenor voice grew vibrant, his mobile features came alight with an earnest passion. Henry Shaw, sitting a few feet away, was awed by what he heard:

> He took the jury by storm. There were tears in Mr. Lincoln's eyes while he spoke. But they were genuine. His sympathies were fully enlisted in favor of the young man, and his terrible sincerity could not but arouse the same passion in the jury. I have said it a hundred times, that it was Lincoln's *speech* that saved that criminal from the gallows, and neither money nor fame inspired that speech, but it was incited by gratitude to the young man's father . . .

As seldom or never before in a courtroom, Lincoln allowed himself to be carried away, this final part of his closing argument lasting, according to Walker, for as long as fifteen minutes. "Such was the power and earnestness with which he spoke," Walker said later, "that jury & all sat as if entranced, & when he was through found relief in a gush of tears."

From where he sat in the jury box, John Brady looked out over the hushed spectators and took special note of Hannah's reaction. Like all the others in the room she'd been swept away: "Tears were plentifully shed by everyone present. The mother of Duff wore a large sun-bonnet; her face was scarcely visible, but her feelings were plainly shown by her sobs."

Contemporary print titled "Lincoln defending Young Armstrong," reflecting public interest in the trial during the 1860 presidential campaign. At the trial Lincoln was clean-shaven, however, not growing a beard until after his election.

The court instructs the jury.

That if they have any reasonable doubt as to whether Metzker came to his death by the blow on the eye, or by the blow on the back of the head, they are to find the defendant "Not guilty" unless they also believe from the evidence, beyond reasonable doubt, that Armstrong and Norris acted by concert, against Metzker, and that Norris struck the blow on the back of the head.

That if they believe from the evidence that Norris killed Metzker, they are to acquit Armstrong, unless they also believe beyond a reasonable doubt that Armstrong acted in concert with Norris in the killing, or purpose to kill or hurt Metzker—

Given [written twice in left margin]

Additional jury instructions suggested by Lincoln, written in his own hand. The word given written twice along the left margin was added by Judge Harriott. Below: the 15-word verdict of the jury clearing Duff Armstrong of all charges, written and signed by jury foreman Milton Logan.

We the Jury, acquit the Defendant from all charges preferred against him in the Indictment.

Milton Logan foreman

The judge's instructions to the jury were brief, but meticulously phrased, and included two propositions asked for by Lincoln. His gaze fixed solemnly on the attentive jurymen, Judge Harriott said that if they believed from the evidence that Armstrong struck the blow as charged, and believed that that same blow caused Metzger's death, then they were bound to find the defendant guilty of first-degree murder. But to reach that verdict they must also believe from the evidence that Armstrong had acted "without any considerable provocation," lack of sufficient cause being enough to "imply malice" in Armstrong's motive. The portion of the judge's instructions that Lincoln had to worry about was the clause allowing for conviction on a reduced charge: the jury "may acquit the defendant Armstrong of the charge of murder and find him guilty of manslaughter," and if so, "they will fix the time of his confinement in the Penitentiary at any [length of] time not exceeding eight years." At the Norris trial that same statement to the jury had brought conviction.

Lincoln's addition to the judge's instructions he wrote out himself and the manuscript survives. It addressed the critical point of collusion, and also spotlighted his contention that the blow to the head by Norris *alone* was the cause of death, as well as emphasizing that the two assailants had not acted together. It was also meant, in the event of a conviction, to make easier an appeal. It consisted of two short paragraphs:

The court instructs the jury that if they have any reasonable doubt as to whether Metzger came to his death by the blow on the eye or the blow on the back of the head, they are to find the defendant not guilty, unless they further believe from the evidence, beyond all reasonable doubt, that Armstrong and Norris acted in concert against Metzger, and that Norris struck the blow on the back of the head.

That if they believe from the evidence that Norris killed Metzger, they are to acquit Armstrong unless they also believe from the evidence, beyond a reasonable doubt, that Armstrong acted in concert with Norris in the killing or purpose to kill or hurt Metzger.

Considering the remarkable denouement provided by Lincoln's passionate peroration, perhaps the only surprising thing about the trial's ending is that the jury took a whole hour to reach a verdict. That hour Lincoln spent waiting in the lobby of a nearby hotel accompanied by the Armstrongs, all except Hannah who preferred to walk off by herself in a pasture back of the courthouse. At last came a hasty summons by the court clerk, and Lincoln called to Hannah but she said she'd rather wait for the news out where she was, alone. The others hurried back to the courtroom in time to watch the twelve filing back into the jury box.

In reply to Judge Harriott's inquiry, jury foreman Milton Logan rose and with evident satisfaction read from a small slip of paper: "We the jury acquit the defendant from all charges preferred against him in the indictment."

Standing at the defense table, a smiling Lincoln extended a large, rough hand, which Duff, standing beside him and wearing an even broader smile, eagerly grasped. Together the two presented a picture of extremes, the white-suited, craggy-faced, six-foot-four lawyer towering above the beaming, pink-cheeked, five-foot-four client.

Calling a man over, Lincoln sent him running to tell Hannah. The sky was just graying, with a few shafts of sunlight still lingering in the hills to the west of Beardstown. Probably Hannah, looking through her tears, was the only one to notice.

FOUR

THE ONE WHO WENT TO JAIL

Six months of brooding in his cell in the penitentiary at Joliet, some two hundred miles northeast of Beardstown, left James Norris a sorely disheartened man, much worried about the little family he'd left on its own back in Mason County. Then, unexpectedly, came the news of Duff's victory—downright startling to Norris it must have been—and his hopes soared. For some unknown reason, however, the particulars of the Armstrong trial, details of the evidence, were very slow in reaching him. That, at least, is the clear implication of an unpublished letter he wrote Lincoln asking for his help in getting his own conviction reviewed or the case retried.

For Norris, approaching Lincoln was an obvious move, inevitable, and yet, as the letter's date shows, more than a year had already passed since the proceedings at Beardstown:

Prison, Joliet, Ills.
Aug 21/59

A. Lincoln Esqr.
A short time since I received a letter from my brother-in-law who informs me that Allen's evidence against me was com-

pletely riddled and he thinks public opinion is now much in my favor. I would like for you to take hold of my case and try if you cannot do something for me. I can secure you one hundred dollars if you think you can do anything. For you cleared Armstrong of the same charge [and] you of course understand the case better than anyone else. If you will take the case in hand you will please address Mr. W. Haines of Havana Ills who will secure you the money.

Please inform me what you can do.

Yours etc
James H. Norris
Care of James Congdon Esqr
Joliet Ills

Though it is a bit inept and rather naive—plunging into the subject as if Lincoln should instantly recognize him and remember the circumstances of the case—the letter shows Norris to have been literate and intelligent. Its most curious feature, of course, is the way he doesn't hesitate to make his offer of $100 to a man who, by then, had become a principal actor on the national stage (a direct result of the famous debates with Douglas in the months following the Armstrong trial), and was already being mentioned for president. What the eager Norris couldn't know was how hopeless his request really was, quite apart from Lincoln's dramatically changed political standing. The one thing that Lincoln now could *never* do was encourage or aid in getting the Norris case reviewed.

If Lincoln ever replied to Norris, his letter, along with any possible reference to it, has so far escaped discovery. A reply, in any case, no matter how gently phrased, could only have been a decided *no*. Given Lincoln's handling of Duff's defense, the decision could not have been otherwise without again endangering Duff. Allen's testimony hadn't really been "riddled," as Norris' brother-in-law reported. That effect or impression was a result of some well-executed legal legerdemain, the work of a master in the art of cross-examination (which Lincoln was conceded to be by every lawyer who watched him handle a witness). It had worked, all right, but only as the arresting climax or centerpiece of all that had preceded it, a patient build-up within the walls of a specific courtroom during a single day's dramatic action.

Further, the fatal blow delivered to Metzger's head by Norris was a vital part of Armstrong's defense. Clearing Norris of guilt for that vicious act, even if it were possible, would be to call in question literally every aspect of the Armstrong evidence, perhaps leading to a revival of the original charge. So twisted, so baroque a legal situation could hardly be explained in words without causing the whole fabric to unravel. No wonder Lincoln never replied.

None of this was guessed by Norris as he waited in his jail cell for the answer that never came. If he didn't know it beforehand, then very soon after writing his letter he must have become aware of the Lincoln-for-president boom, starting slowly but quickly catching fire. At least by then he knew he needn't look for a reply.

Yet, eventually, something *was* done for Norris, something that, judging by all the rules of evidence, had in it the quietly manipulating hand of President Lincoln himself. Surviving documents in the matter are scanty—and a few documents that should be there are missing—but they prove beyond doubt something never yet suspected, that Lincoln from the White House silently engineered a pardon for Norris. It took time and effort and needed the quiet cooperation of three old associates of Lincoln's, but it got done. Even a president had to observe the proprieties in such things, especially if he wished, as Lincoln certainly did, to remain anonymous.

The wheels were set going in the fall of 1861, when Norris had been in prison some four years and Lincoln in office as president barely six months. Involved was a rather tangled process, starting with Lincoln's longtime friend and political colleague Richard Yates, then governor of Illinois.

Previously Yates had served as head of an Illinois railroad, the

Prison, Joliet, Ills Aug 24/59
A Lincoln Esqr:
                    A short time
Since I received a letter from my
brother-in-law who informs me
that Allen's evidence against me
was completely riddled and he
thinks public opinion is now much
in my favor. I would like for you to
take hold of my case and try if you
cannot do something for me. I can
secure you one hundred dollars if
you think you can do anything.
For you cleared Armstrong of the
same charge you of course understand the case better than any one
else. If you will take the case in
hand you will please address
Mr W. Haines. Havanna Ills who
will secure you the Money

1841

Unpublished letter to Lincoln written by Duff Armstrong's accomplice in the killing, James Norris. Convicted separately of manslaughter, and then serving an eight-year sentence in the state penitentiary, Norris here asks Lincoln to reopen his case. No reply by Lincoln is known.

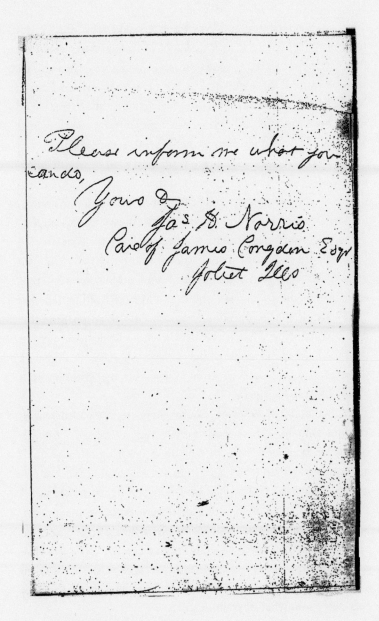

Please inform me what you
can do,
    Yours &
        Jas. D. Norris.
    Care of James Congdon Esqr
            Joliet Ills

Page two of the Norris letter to Lincoln.

Tonica and Petersburg Line. When he left to take office as governor in January 1861, into his vacated spot at the railroad moved the firm's number two man, none other than William G. Greene. This was the same Billy Green (the final e came later) whom Lincoln had known well back in his New Salem days, the same friend who'd been the principal arranger in setting up the wrestling bout with Jack Armstrong. Prospering in real estate and banking, Greene too had come a long way, was now a man of wealth enjoying a certain position of influence in the state. At Lincoln's direction (the only reasonable conclusion given all the circumstances) he now arranged for a formal petition to be drawn up and submitted to Governor Yates, asking executive clemency for Norris.

It was not a difficult matter to accomplish. Many of the residents of Mason County, Norris' own friends and relatives and others who had heard or read about the Metzger killing, felt that Duff's acquittal also proved the innocence of his companion that night. Certainly to a hasty judgment that would seem an obvious conclusion from the nature of the evidence offered at Beardstown. But in any case, it was felt, if Armstrong got off then it was only fair to do the same for Norris.

With the aid of a Mason County man he knew well named William Pelham, Greene had the petition completed and fully signed by October 15. He then wrote a covering letter to Yates introducing Pelham with his petition. An old neighbor of his, Pelham was a worthy, honest man who'd explain all about the case: "I am not personally familiar with the circumstances of the murder. So far as I can learn, the community where the difficulty occurred seem to think that Norris has fully attoned & ought to be set at liberty." None of this, it can confidently be said, would have taken Yates unaware. Certainly he'd been well prepared through other channels about what was coming.

One further item now falls into place, removing any least hesitation as to President Lincoln's involvement. William Herndon, then staunchly carrying on the partners' law business in Springfield, contributed a written note of his own to the petition documents. Strongly and openly—though in curiously abrupt fashion—he presses Yates to grant the clemency asked for, and to do so *promptly*: "Mr. Pelham, a citizen of Mason Co. wishes to see you. If possible see him and grant his prayer as quickly as circumstances will admit of etc." Yates, of course, didn't need to be told that behind Herndon's perfunctory request lay Lincoln's personal endorsement, that is, didn't need to be told that Herndon was writing *on behalf* of Lincoln, was acting in the matter at Lincoln's explicit direction. This is easily shown, for Herndon himself had not the least involvement in the Armstrong case. Strangely, he had never even discussed it with his partner, a fact sufficiently proved by his sole subsequent reference to it. A single, lengthy paragraph in his 1889 biography of Lincoln, it offers nothing new, but merely retails the information supplied long before by the attorney Henry Shaw and Hannah Armstrong. He also gets dead wrong the whole business about the witness Allen and the moon, blandly stating that Lincoln in cross-examining Allen proved "from an almanac that the moon had set." Again, if Herndon had had the least hint of the truth of Watkins' testimony he would never have written as he does in his biography of his partner that Lincoln would not under any circumstances "sacrifice truth or right in the slightest degree for the love of a friend."

The written petition handed Yates by Pelham was a lengthy one carrying no fewer than 148 signatures. Among the signers, besides Greene himself, were two Armstrongs (but not Duff), and five men who had acted as witnesses at the trial, either for the prosecution or the defense. A half-dozen other signers are familiar as having known and been good friends with Lincoln at New Salem: such substantial citizens as Abram and Jacob Bale, Russell Godbey, James Short, and Royal Clary.

The relevant portion of the petition makes fairly precise mention of both trials, its main point of pleading being much the expected one:

... but one man, Allen, saw the commission of the deed. Other men, among whom are some of your petitioners, were said by the said Allen to have been present as well as himself, witnessed nothing of the kind, and have so testified in open court in the said Norris's case and also in the case of the People vs Armstrong, who was implicated by the same witness, tried at Beardstown and found "not guilty.["] In addition to this, the said Allen was proven to have been present on a different part of the campground long after the time which the witnesses fixed as the time of the commission of the offense. Norris is a man of family having a wife and three [four] children who are in a destitute condition, depending on charity for their support . . .

No doubt exists in the mind of the undersigned that Allen, the only witness for the prosecution—except some physicians who only testified as to the nature of the wounds which Metzger the deceased received—was either wholly and entirely mistaken in point of fact or testified wilfully and corruptly false in each material particular. We petition for the unconditional pardon of the said James H. Norris and believe the act would be doing justice to an innocent man, an act worthy of the highest praise and admiration, all of which we humbly submit in connection with the sworn statements herewith sent for your serious consideration.

Among the documents missing from the pardon file are those very "sworn statements" emphasized in the petition, an unfortunate loss, for they may have had a bearing on the unexpected outcome: for whatever reason, Yates denied the petition. No existing record tells why he disallowed it, and only a single phrase inked on the outside of the original petition preserves the fact that he did so: "Application *vetoed*. See enclosure." What the enclosure may have been is also unknown, for it too has disappeared from the file.

W. G. GREENE, Pres.
JAS. BERDAN, Treas. & Sec.
W. T. BEEKMAN, Supt.
WM. BACON, Gen'l Agt.

OFFICE OF THE

Tonica & Petersburg R. R. Co.

Home Oct 15th 1861

Hon Richard Yates

Dear Sir

W. C. Pelam

The bearer of this visits you for the purpos
of getting a certain Mr Norice released
from further confinement in the Peni
-tentiary Mr Pelam is a reliable worthy
man I usit to live near him in Mason
he can give you the the Circumstance
of the Criminals guilt or inocence
I am not personaly familiar with the
circumstance of the Murder sofar as I
can learn the Community where the
dificulty occurred seme to think that Norris
has fully attoned & ought to be set at
liberty having been in the Penitentiary now
four years. I would recommend him to your
Clemency. Yours truly   W C Greene

Unpublished letter of William Greene, another old New Salem friend of Lincoln's and a business colleague of Illinois Governor Richard Yates, to Governor
Yates asking him to receive a pardon petition on behalf of James Norris.

Unpublished note of Lincoln's law partner William Herndon to Illinois governor Richard Yates, a friend and political ally of Lincoln, urging him to grant a pardon to Norris. Herndon had no connection with the Armstrong case and is here acting at the direction of Lincoln, then occupying the White House.

A year went by, for Norris and his family no doubt a very slow year—though being in prison did keep him from the hazards of military service at a time when the Union was fighting, and mostly losing, some very hard battles. When the question of a pardon again came up it began with another letter to Governor Yates, this one directly from the prisoner. Comparing it with the letter Norris wrote Lincoln earlier, it is clear that he had help in writing it, confirming the suspicion that the idea for a second approach also came from the outside.

Of course, with the war going badly for the North, it was not a good time for a convicted felon to be asking for help with his individual problem. Yates, for one, a rabid Unionist who declared his willingness to "wade through seas of blood" rather than let the South depart, had his hands full with the war effort in his own state, mainly the enormous task of equipping troops for the field. In addition, he was seriously feuding with Lincoln over several important matters. The agonizingly slow pace of the war on the North's part, for instance, distressed him greatly, as it did many others. There was also his incessant demand for military commissions and promotions for Illinois troops, the rank of general in particular. "Generalships in the Regular army," replied the exasperated Lincoln at one point, "are not as plenty as blackberries!"

When the Norris letter reached Yates' office early in March 1863 his mind was dealing with topics far removed from courts and prisons:

Ills State Prison
Feb 22/63

Gov. R. Yates
Springfield, Ills.
Sir:
It is with feelings of the most profound emotion that I venture to address you, feelings of such a nature that I scarce know in what terms to write you; my best plan however will

be to give your excellency a slight sketch of my case, and then you can judge whether I have been sufficiently punished or not.

In August "57" I together with a man named Wm Armstrong was charged with killing a man in Mason Co. Ill., of which offense I am as completely innocent as the babe unborn. I was placed in jail and at that time had a wife and 4 small children completely dependent upon me for support. I had no means whatsoever to fee Counsel with, and under these circumstances was desirous of procuring a trial as quick as possible. The presiding judge (whose name was Harriott) appointed me as Counsel a gentleman named Wm Walker, a young man inexperienced at the bar, & opposed to whom was Hugh Fullerton, L. W. Ross, and John Collier, gentlemen of wide experience and great abilities.

Under these unfavorable circumstances it is no wonder that I was convicted of manslaughter and sentenced to States prison for 8 years.

Armstrong procured a change of venue to Cass Co. and there was defended by our President A. Lincoln and by him acquitted, chiefly by breaking down the testimony of one Chas. Allen, said Allen being my sole and only prosecutor. Now Your Excellency it looks very hard that I should have to suffer 8 long years in prison on the oath of a man who was, afterwards, proved to have given false testimony in the very same case but against a different party.

In Nov. "61" a gentleman named Wm C. Pelham got up a petition in my favor & placed it on file in the Gov's. office where I presume it still is. Pelham went to the war and got killed, and now I have got no one to attend to the case for me; under these circumstances I humbly beg and pray of your Excellency to look into my case, and if in your judgment I have been wronged to use your Executive authority in my behalf and have me released from my imprisonment.

Three Lincoln colleagues and friends who, acting for President Lincoln, quietly engineered a pardon for the convicted killer James Norris. (L. to r.) William Greene, Governor Richard Yates, William Herndon. None of the three had a personal link to the case.

If you require a letter of recommendation from this place I can procure you one, showing that I have conducted myself in a proper and becoming manner since my incarceration. Will your Excellency please answer this and let me know your determination—

> With Great Respect
> Yr. Humble Servant
> James H. Norris

Too busy to respond or take action, Yates allowed four months to pass before contacting the lawyer, William Walker, named in the letter. On July 10, 1863, a two-page letter arrived from Walker, setting out the facts of the case as he recalled them. The claim that the witness Charles Allen had been elsewhere on the campgrounds when the fight occurred was repeated, along with Armstrong's advantage in having an extra six months to prepare, and again stressing Lincoln's part in the trial. The acquittal of Armstrong, said Walker, "made everybody feel that Norris was wrongfully convicted. I have thought so all the time I was in each case, and I feel sure that had we on the trial of Norris the same testimony that we had on the trial of Armstrong, he would never [have] been where he is." If Yates was curious as to why something hadn't been done sooner, "I can only answer by saying that Norris was a poor man and no one seemed willing to move in the matter."

(The last comment seems to point to Walker's ignorance of the 1861 petition for pardon submitted under the guidance of Greene and Herndon. *Why* he didn't know, being himself a Mason County resident as well as a part of the original case, is a question probably now beyond answering. That he might for some reason in his letter to Yates be dissembling is possible, if unlikely.)

Less than a month after reading Walker's letter, Yates at last found the time to act, or say he at last proved willing to move in the matter. On August 7 he sent a note to O. M. Hatch, Illinois secretary of state: "Please issue pardon to James H. Norris as prayed in the within papers." With that, Norris walked free, three years short of his original sentence. Yates' reason for finally releasing him, where earlier he'd refused, is nowhere stated.

Here Norris disappears from the record of the case. Returning to his family in Mason County, he lived at least another dozen years, and probably much more than that. He was still alive when the story of Lincoln and the Armstrong affair began to gain public attention, yet he is never heard from, was not sought out by reporters or historians. The last traceable sign of him is to be found in some papers in the Havana courthouse. They show that he and his wife Eliza were divorced in 1873, she and her four children by then having lived apart from him for many years.

Of peculiar interest is the fate of Norris' original 1859 prison letter to Lincoln, asking for his help. Neither lost nor destroyed, it was for a long time entirely beyond the reach of historians—more by accident than on purpose, it appears.

Left in the files of his Springfield law office when Lincoln went to Washington, it later became mixed with the vast horde of his presidential papers. At Lincoln's death this entire collection was immediately sequestered from public view by his son Robert, to spare any possible embarrassment to living persons, as he explained. It was not until 1947, twenty-one years after Robert's death, that the collection was at last unsealed. By then the celebrated Almanac Trial, as it came to be called, had taken its place as an integral part of Lincoln biography, by far his best-known case as a lawyer. But Norris' part in it had nearly faded out, a barely discernible face in an old sepia photograph.

Concerning Norris' immensely crucial if silent role in the Armstrong trial, there remained little more than his name and his conviction. Unlike Duff, he had no relative or friend willing to come forward to describe or defend his role in the famous case, at least none ever did. Nor has any later historian or Lincoln scholar been moved to ask why, on the same evidence or nearly so, one man went to prison while another went free.

Just short of a century after it was written the Norris letter to Lincoln became freely available to all, nestled among the many thousands of documents in the Lincoln collection at the Library of Congress. For another half-century now it has continued to rest there, unpublished and unremarked.

FIVE

THE FAKED ALMANAC

Among the twelve men who sat on the Armstrong jury there was at least one whose politics were the opposite of Lincoln's, an avowed Democrat who preferred the policies of Stephen Douglas. In the senatorial campaign pitting Lincoln against Douglas that began some two months after the trial, this man, never identified, became the initial source of the most peculiar legend to adorn the Lincoln saga. Widely circulated at the time as a discredit to the candidate, it was revived for the presidential campaign of 1860, and has been much talked about ever since, its truth or accuracy seemingly still a question with some.

The clever but unscrupulous Springfield lawyer, it was said, had secretly altered the almanac he used so dramatically at the trial, physically changed words and numbers on the page to make the data support his argument about the moon. So deftly was it done, supposedly, and so subtly presented in court, that none at the time had guessed the daring imposture.

Once started, no matter how often denied or by whom, there was little possibility of halting such a story or of preventing the many convolutions it afterwards underwent—the principal addition being that he had doctored an almanac for a year other than

1857. Outright rejection of the charge, by people aware of Lincoln's reputation for upright dealing, quickly surfaced. Yet there were many even among the well-disposed, Lincoln supporters and reverers of his memory, who in the absence of evidence either way confessed themselves undecided. To compound matters, the story's first authoritative appearance in print came from the hands of one of Lincoln's oldest and closest friends, a man who went to Washington with him and often acted as the president's good right hand, Ward Lamon. Only seven years after Lincoln's death, Lamon's biography of him was published and with that the strange episode of the faked almanac became indelibly fixed in Lincoln lore. At a certain level of popular perception, and even to some extent at higher levels, it is still believed, at least thought possible.

After describing the murder of Metzger and the evidence against the attackers almost airily, as if there were no doubt of its truth, Lamon slides into the topic. He doesn't linger over the details and gets the nub of the original moon story wrong. Yet in a curious way his offhand treatment only adds to its seeming authenticity:

> . . . it is easy to pervert and even to destroy evidence like this; and here Mr. Lincoln saw an opportunity which nobody had dreamed of in the Norris trial. He handed to an officer of the court an almanac, and told him to give it back to him when he should call for it in the presence of the jury. It was an almanac of the year previous to the murder . . .
>
> In due time he called for the almanac, and easily proved by it that, at the time the main witness claimed the moon was shining in great splendor, there was in fact no moon at all, but black darkness over the whole scene. In the "roar of laughter" and undisguised astonishment succeeding this apparent demonstration, court, jury, and counsel forgot to examine that seemingly conclusive almanac, and let it pass without a question concerning its genuineness.

In reality, Lamon himself knew nothing personally of any falsified document of any sort used at the trial. Like everyone else he'd heard the stories that were circulating before and after Lincoln's death in 1865, then he gained access to the letter of Henry Shaw written to William Herndon commenting on the trial. What he says about the almanac was picked up bodily from Shaw, but he entirely misses, or purposely ignores, Shaw's unsure, meandering tone and attitude. Confusedly, Shaw says that the almanac was "of the year previous to the murder," then adds that he thought *two* almanacs were brought into the court, one for 1857 the other for 1856, and he ends by declaring that Lincoln "was entirely innocent of any deception." He also says that he spoke with jury foreman Milton Logan who declared himself "willing to make an affidavit" that the almanac was the correct one, for 1857 (the Logan affidavit was actually made, later to be seen by Judge Bergen). To these mitigating points, Lamon paid no attention.

Himself an experienced lawyer and respected colleague of Lincoln's in many cases on the circuit, how Lamon could believe or accept the laughable idea that all the experienced legal minds in the court at Beardstown "forgot to examine" the supposedly spurious volume, is a wonder. It tells a great deal in fact, about the status of the legend at the time, for Lamon was not introducing the story or even explaining it, only confirming it (his book was ghostwritten but Lamon approved everything).

Bearing Lamon's seal of approval, the story thereafter steadily grew in complexity and drama until it could be soberly stated that Lincoln capped his forgery by buying up all the genuine almanacs in town so his trick wouldn't be discovered. Or that under cover of night on arriving in Beardstown he stole quietly "into a drug-store at the corner of the square on State Street," bought several copies of an 1858 almanac—or 1853 or 1854—and back in his room at the Dunbaugh House changed all the dates and other tell-tale features. Or that while cross-examining Allen he suddenly paused and sent someone running out to buy an almanac that he had prepared and somehow planted at that same drug store. Sixty years later, Beardstown residents would "confidently point out the drug-store, still in operation."

About 1890 the burgeoning legend took a sudden new twist when an old almanac was found—so it was claimed—among the papers of Henry Shaw who had died several years before. Study showed that its year, originally 1853, had been altered to 1857, with similar changes throughout. No publicity accompanied the find and it was soon sold, going to a private collector in Chicago. About 1920 it reached the Chicago Historical Society, where it came under the searching eye of the prominent Lincoln scholar William Barton, who in curiously clumsy fashion proceeded to make it an issue.

Though it should have been starkly clear to Barton—to anyone who could spare a moment to think—that in the circumstances of the trial a doctored almanac was an absurdity, his scholarly detachment and thoroughness impelled him to make a detailed inspection of the curious object. With magnifying glass and even a microscope he poured over the brittle, yellowed pages one by one looking for evidence to settle the question either way. What he found left him only with a head spinning in confusion, or so he made it sound in his report—not deliberately, of course.

"An almanac is in existence," he begins uncertainly, "which claims to be the one Lincoln used. It is an almanac ingeniously made over from one of the year 1853. If that almanac was the one really used, a fraud was perpetrated on the court." However, he has personally examined the volume and feels sure that Lincoln did not use "this fraudulent almanac." His reasons, mainly, are his firm faith in Lincoln's honesty, plus the added fact that Lincoln was always much too cautious of his reputation to risk exposure in that way (reasons not at all well matched!). In a further display of naiveté, he adds that Lincoln didn't need tricks to win the case, for he was certain "of his ability to influence a jury with the kindness of Duff Armstrong's parents to him when a poor boy."

Then, insists Barton, there is the strange artifact itself. Much too well done to be the product of a night's hasty invention, it was at the same time too poorly done to fool its intended target: "In every case the date is changed with type, a character 7 being used after a knife had been employed in scratching . . . Every page where the changes have been made shows when held to the light that the paper has been scraped . . . it is hardly possible that some one of the twelve jurors would not have detected the imposture." He adds that it was even less possible that the judge would have allowed so obvious a fraud to be entered in evidence.

Worse, besides the outright physical tampering, the forger had left the days of the week as they stood in 1853. August 29 for instance, showed as a Monday, where in 1857 it was a Saturday, a fact by the time of the trial well known to all.

"Did Lincoln do it?" asks Barton suddenly, opening up the question again even as his reader has begun to feel that it was settled. Did he get somebody else to do it? Was he imposed upon? "This is not likely," explains Barton. "It would not have been easy to deceive so astute a man as Mr. Lincoln with this almanac. If Mr. Lincoln used this, he may be presumed to have prepared it or at least to have accepted it with the full knowledge of the use to which it was adapted." Here the head of Barton's reader commences spinning.

After all his lurching about, Barton concludes by stating his own belief as to where the almanac actually used by Lincoln—the authoritative, undoctored one—came from, and how. With Allen on the witness stand, he says, Lincoln "sent Jacob Jones, a cousin of Armstrong's, across the corner to the drug-store. Jones brought back the almanac, and Lincoln found the place and passed it to the judge." Barton actually believed, it seems, that Lincoln would have come to the trial without bringing with him a copy of the almanac, trusting that he'd find one for sale at the drug store! Or perhaps he here accepts the older version of the tale in which the business about the moon comes to Lincoln in a flash as he questions Allen. It's hard to be sure.

The conscientious Barton was not the man for a technical study of this sort—a fake fake!—so that the unintended result of his work for many readers was to make the legend appear intriguingly possible. In other ways, over and over, Barton had already proved his sterling worth to the Lincoln saga, his value in research and interpretation. Here, sadly, he became, as with Lamon earlier, a principal means of fixing the strange almanac legend fast in the public mind. Staunchly intending to deny and reject it, he lost his way in a thicket of unfamiliar detail, as have so many others.

Much more relevant than hunting up old almanacs was the work of those few who inquired what astronomy might have to tell of conditions in the sky that night. If the moon on August 29, 1857, in Mason County, Illinois, really had set on or about midnight—if when the fight took place the moon had been sitting right on the horizon, ready to dip out of sight below it—then there would have been no need for Lincoln to play with the facts. To demonstrate Allen's error as to the moon's position he had only to place in evidence any of the half-dozen standard almanacs available to him.

Lamon (or his ghostwriter) was the first to make the effort, a weak one. He merely inquired of an official at the *Nautical Almanac* in Washington D.C., and was told that moonset in Cass County for August 29, 1857 had occurred just about midnight, actually three minutes before. This information Lamon, without comment, demoted to a footnote in his book, paying it no further attention. J. N. Gridley, author of the important 1910 article on the Armstrong case, came next. He applied to the astronomy department at the University of Illinois and was given a slightly different time for moonset, five minutes after midnight. Biographer Barton in 1921 put the question to three leading observatories and all three agreed on five minutes past midnight. In 1928 another prominent Lincoln scholar, Albert Beveridge, queried the Harvard Observatory and was told the same: 12:05 A.M. on August 30.

More recently (1990), two physicists at a Texas university made the numbers even more precise, shaving off a full minute to 12:04 on the thirtieth. Then they added an interesting new note to the puzzle by pointing out a fact till then overlooked, that in lunar terms 1857 had been quite unusual. Culminating a regular lunar cycle of 18.6 years, the year 1857 saw the moon attain extreme positions in relation to the earth, "running high" as it moved through the heavens, then days later "running low." On August 15 it ran high. Two weeks later, on the very night of the murder, it ran uncommonly low, reaching almost minus-thirty degrees, "nearly the extreme value [of declination] which the moon can possibly attain."

A waxing, gibbous moon (between half and full, and growing), on the twenty-ninth it traveled from meridian to moonset with comparative speed, taking little more than four hours. This exceptional situation, explain the two physicists, offers a possible reason for the discrepancy between what Allen said about the moon's position at the time of the fight (nearly overhead), and the undeniable fact that moonset took place an hour later. The unusual trajectory presented the glowing, three-quarters moon in full view one moment and—so to speak—gone the next, having rapidly dropped toward the horizon. In turn, say the two authors, that fact also helps to explain how the faked almanac legend was born. Perhaps it does, to an extent. But the true genesis of the legend is more complicated than that, involving several converging strands.

That the initial charge of fraud came from among the Armstrong jurors was no accident. Sooner or later one of the twelve was bound to awaken to the troubling realization that he'd been hoodwinked by the glib, insinuating defense counsel. Chagrined, he certainly would have asked himself how it had happened.

That a moon had indeed been shining in a clear sky on the night of the twenty-ninth stood undoubted by anyone in either trial—a bright moon shedding its silvery beams full on the Walker's Grove campground. That fact was received as true because it *was* true. The almanac proved it. Only when Lincoln in cross-examining Allen made it a point of contention did anyone pause to think about the moon at all. But Lincoln's subtle art, by focusing on the moon's *position*, did more than impugn the credibility of a witness. It also left the impression, mistaken but indelible, that he had at the same time disproved Allen's claim as to the scene being well lighted. With that, the chief witness against Armstrong, the man most responsible for Norris' conviction, was virtually eliminated. That victory, when combined with the evidence of Watkins and Dr. Parker, made acquittal certain. Lincoln's impassioned summation was insurance.

Later, with time to think, the jurymen in particular would have been puzzled to understand how the moon had become the central question. Low in the sky or up high, there *had* been a moon and it had given *plenty* of light. The witness Allen could easily have seen the crime being committed, as he swore under oath. If Lincoln with his almanac had managed to prove the opposite, then there seemed only one explanation: the almanac, though inspected by judge, jury, and prosecutors, must have been in some way wrong. From there a leap to a certain conclusion was unavoidable: Lincoln had introduced doctored evidence, practicing fraud on the court. In the nature of the case that meant a deftly faked almanac, inevitably with Lincoln himself as fabricator—a charge his political opponents wouldn't hesitate to make but would be quite happy to get hold of in even embryonic form, promptly enlarging it. Honest Abe a forger!

Adding to this air of fraud in the later recollections of at least some of the jury was the sudden bustle they had witnessed in court as the almanac was being introduced. To everyone's surprise, Lincoln begins handing round the three copies of *Jayne's*. Then comes the questioning, and then the explosion of laughter at the disconcerted Allen's expense. Quickly there follows the action of the suspicious Fullerton, who dispatches a man to gather up more almanacs. The departure of this messenger, of course, explains all the later claims about Lincoln, or someone sent by him, buying almanacs in the local drug store. If none were to be had in the courthouse, the messenger may even have hurried outside to get one, or a second one by another publisher.

Next comes the whispered huddle at the prosecution's table as the different volumes are compared. Easily forgotten by the jurors afterward was the total absence of any challenge by Fullerton to admitting the almanac in evidence. To assume, as the legend does, that the experienced and respected state's attorney could have been fooled by surreptitious alterations in a printed document, and would have failed to test such evidence by all means possible, is merely silly. This absence of a challenge by Fullerton, when Lincoln cited the almanac, is the final proof that the almanac was genuine.

A prime example—because it was offered so casually—of the vaguely confused process by which these separate elements flowed together to form the enduring legend of the faked almanac is seen in a stray newspaper account of about 1895. It gives comment by elderly Mason County locals on the fact that Duff Armstrong, then still living, always insisted fiercely that the Lincoln almanac was genuine:

Uncle Johnny Potter, who was an intimate friend of the Armstrongs, laughed and shook his head when asked what the real facts were. It seems that after the trial the friends of the Armstrongs talked the matter over. Some of them remembered as positively as the witnesses had done that there was nearly a full moon on the night Press Metzger was beaten at the camp meeting. They insisted on their recollections in spite of Mr. Lincoln's documentary evidence.

There was an overhauling of old almanacs in various households. Sure enough, they showed a moon nearly in mid-heavens at the hour of the affray. Then there was inquiry for the almanac which had been presented by Mr. Lincoln in court. The little pamphlet could not be found.

Very probably these people, talking among themselves of an event which lay within their own youthful experience, really did take the trouble to look up some old almanacs. If so, then it's true of course that they would have found full support for their forty-year-old memories, though not in quite the way they remembered or that is pictured by the clipping. "Nearly a full moon" is close enough to the actual gibbous stage at the hour of the fight. But "nearly in mid-heavens" to describe the moon's position is way off. Yet there is a reason for that phrase—an echo of Allen's testimony, of course. It stands for the crucial fact that the moon had *not set*, that while low, it was still high enough, and bright enough, to illuminate the ugly attack on the hulking Metzger by his two diminutive but liquored and well-armed opponents.

It is also true that the "little pamphlet," the original almanac used by Lincoln, could not be found, then or since. Whatever happened to it, or to either of the other two copies that Lincoln presented in court, is not known. Aside from the obvious hoax investigated by Barton, no collector or dealer has ever claimed to possess one, certainly not the veritable, unaltered copy Lincoln read from in court. That is a situation at least mildly curious—arguing a sad dearth of enterprising forgers!—since a simple signature, *A. Lincoln*, inked on a genuine copy of a *Jayne's*, a *Goudy's*, or an *Ayer's* for 1857, would be very hard to disprove. Perhaps that is the problem, however, for the flimsy booklets, meant to be replaced annually, were printed on the cheapest paper and wouldn't have lasted long. Only a few copies of each can be found today, all preserved in the special collections and rare book departments of certain public and university libraries. The familiar *Old Farmer's Almanac*, widely used at the time, apparently is not a candidate for the honor, being mentioned nowhere in the sources for the Armstrong case.

The only other relic of the trial that might still survive, aside from the original court documents, is the wicked slung-shot used so cruelly by Duff. Exhibited to the jury in court, that same day it was presented by Lincoln as a gift to his opposing counsel, Henry Shaw. "Here, Henry, I'll give you this to remember me by," Shaw quotes Lincoln as saying as he handed him the weapon at the conclusion of the trial. "I have that same slung-shot now," he adds. Shaw died in 1885, but the slung-shot apparently didn't turn up in his estate, and nothing has been heard of it since.

In passing, concerning the slung-shot a final question might be asked. How is it that Lincoln felt able to dispose so blithely of an important item of state's evidence? Found by Mason County investigators on the campgrounds soon after Metzger's killing, the slung-shot stayed in the sheriff's custody until the trial, of course being in the meantime made available to both sides for examination. Does Lincoln's assumption that, with the trial ended, he could simply give it away to whomever he pleased reflect the admittedly looser legal protocol of that time and place? Perhaps it does. Still, the action seems peculiar. It remains one of the minor puzzles of the Almanac Trial.

SNAPSHOTS

The lanky, white-suited Lincoln, walking from the courthouse back along Beardstown's main street to his hotel, made a conspicuous figure. People he passed stared briefly trying to think who it might be. Some, perhaps, knowing that the Armstrong trial had just concluded, and having seen pictures of the Springfield lawyer, guessed the truth. One who did was Abram Byers, a local photographer who on spotting Lincoln, decided to ask for a sitting. Celebrity photos were good for business, helping to draw in ordinary customers, and if Lincoln did run for the U.S. Senate against the nationally famous Stephen Douglas, there'd be a ready market for copies, as always with the leading politicians. From what the papers were saying, his chances looked pretty good.

"This suit's awfully rumpled and it's dirty," replied Lincoln to Byer's invitation. Not at all, insisted the photographer, even though the suit probably *was* wrinkled and soiled. It looked just fine, said Byers, and anything wrong like that wouldn't show much in the ambrotype process he used. Together the two walked over to Byers' studio on nearby Monroe Street.

Seating Lincoln beside the usual draped table, Byers placed the right arm just so, the forearm resting at an angle on the table top, the large, powerful hand tightly grasping the rounded table edge. A half-dozen other studio portraits of Lincoln show him in a similar pose, with his right hand hanging over the table edge. Only in this one does the hand take such a firm grip, the long fingers curled under.

The head Byers didn't set at an angle, in the fashion of other Lincoln photographers most of whom shot a three-quarters view to emphasize the dramatic molding of the features with their precipitous planes and sharp angles. Instead, he instructed the subject to look squarely at the camera, full-face, staring directly into the lens. Then he brushed back the thick, black hair and adjusted the very loose collar to hide the long, stringy neck. The lens was opened, and when it was shut again after some minutes, Byers possessed one of the most unusual of all the hundred or so Lincoln photographs.

Among existing pictures of the beardless, pre-presidential Lincoln, only one or two others show him full-face looking foursquare at the camera, both large ears equally prominent. The facial expression in them is the familiar one of settled strength and quiet self-possession. In the Byers ambrotype, on the other hand, another note is subtly seen, or felt. It is in the eyes mostly, but also in the set of the mouth, the lift of the chin, the slight tilt of the head.

At one instant the viewer sees the simple confidence of an honest man, relaxed and at ease with the world. Then there creeps in a curious sense that behind the unconcern the man has suddenly become defensive, assumed an apprehensive air, as if he'd just remembered something. It is not at all a matter of reading impressions into the portrait, for in another moment both impressions—or say qualities, the tone and timbre of the facial expression—are clearly present, peculiarly blended. The photograph is a remarkable capturing of a remarkable man, standing out all the more because of the rare white suit he so conspicuously wears. Recalling all that the subject had been through in the ten hours just preceding the photo—and the six months before that—it can also be said that it is a remarkably truthful one.

As to the question of why, for his defense of the certainly guilty Duff Armstrong, he chose to wear white, a color he never or almost never wore before (the question can't be settled by existing evidence), no answer is attempted here. It would be far too easy to get swept into the excesses of psychiatric symbolism, and with Lincoln there has already been too much of such groping.

Besides, the answer is rather plain if a bit sad.

What of Duff Armstrong? What became of the lucky young man whose name for the remainder of his life, though he and Lincoln never met again, was inextricably linked with that of his great benefactor?

Duff lived another forty years and married twice, his first wife dying. He fathered five children, and was sixty-three at his second marriage, his new wife being a widow of fifty. When the Civil War started he was twenty-seven years old, and with three of his brothers he enlisted in the 85th Illinois Volunteer Infantry. One brother was killed in battle, and another was wounded. Duff saw no combat and his military record was undistinguished, to say the least. At one point he was officially listed as a deserter but later returned to to his outfit under a general amnesty proclaimed in 1863 for Union deserters by President Lincoln. Soon he fell ill, however, developing crippling rheumatism, and spent the rest of his service in army hospitals.

Here again his mother came boldly to his rescue. In September 1863 Hannah wrote (by the aid of a friend) directly to the White House, begging Lincoln to have her ailing son discharged and sent home to her care. Among Hannah's friends the attempt brought only derisive laughter for its presumption, and even her own family said that it wouldn't work this time. She couldn't expect special treatment for the boy, they said, when so many other distraught mothers had sons in peril. They were wrong. No sooner did Lincoln receive her pleading letter than he took action, personally writing the good news to Hannah: "I have just ordered the discharge of your boy William—as you say now at Louisville KY. A. Lincoln."

Delighted if more than a little surprised, Duff went back to his mother in Mason County where he eventually recovered, again taking up his life as a farmer. Always an object of interest to regional newspapers and local historians (professional historians by then had forgotten all about him), he steadfastly refused to talk with anyone about the old case, brushing off all questioners. Finally in 1896 he gave an interview, a lengthy one, to a local newspaper, but it proves to be full of errors and the sort of distortion to be expected after so many years, and from personal prejudice.* He died in 1899 and is buried in New Hope Cemetery, town of Easton, Mason County.

Hannah's life, too, stretched far past the time of the Metzger trial, gaining new vigor in 1865 when, at the age of fifty-four, she remarried. As Mrs. Samuel Wilcox, she moved west to Iowa, joining a group of relatives and friends already there. With her new husband she settled in Winterset, Madison County, soon becoming a personality in the region because of her peculiar ties with the martyred president. Her old Illinois roots stayed strong, and when she died in 1890 her body was returned to Mason County for burial. She lies in Petersburg cemetery, a few miles from the Concord grave of her first husband.

---

* For the interview in full see Appendix C.

Arriving back in Springfield the day after the Armstrong acquittal, Lincoln promptly took up several law cases that had been waiting his attention. He also began research and study for a long and important speech he'd started writing. If all went well, he'd be called on to deliver it in little more than a month. Containing a large portion of factual matter, it had probably been begun some time before, being interrupted by the Armstrong affair.

For the next few weeks, mid-May to mid-June, he mixed the practice of law with politics, appearing in court perhaps a dozen times, none to try a jury case. Only once did he leave Springfield, and that was for a single day to give "a good Republican speech" at Edwardsville, near St. Louis. Through the first days of June his worry over the possible encroachment of his rival Stephen Douglas lessened a bit, yet never quite went away.

Scheduled for June 16 in Springfield was the Republican state convention, at which the senatorial candidate would be chosen. On the day before, Lincoln convened a small group of his advisers and read them the completed speech, asking for their opinions. No, they all said, it wouldn't do, especially the opening. Much too controversial. A blow-up in the ranks would result, not the best way to start a senatorial campaign, particularly against the formidable Douglas. Can't expect the old-line politicians to listen to inflammable rhetoric like that. At least rewrite the opening they advised, tone it down.

Lincoln thought about it awhile, then said no, he'd stick with what he had. He'd give the speech just the way he'd written it first.

Next day in the State House at Springfield the Republicans of Illinois chose Abraham Lincoln as their candidate for the U.S. Senate. That same evening in the State House he delivered his speech, starting off with a quote from Jesus: "A house divided against itself cannot stand," he said. "I believe this government cannot endure permanently half-slave and half-free. I do not expect the Union to be dissolved. I do not expect the House to fall. But I do expect it will cease to be divided. It will become all one thing or all the other . . ."

By the time Lincoln finished speaking that evening he had taken his first firm step on the two-year path to the presidency. In both of the campaigns that followed—his failed try for the Senate that year, and his victory in 1860—the Armstrong case made its final public appearances when his opponents threw at him the faked almanac charge. If honesty, integrity, was a large part of his appeal, then they'd explore the fraudulent way he had *really* saved his friends' son. Fortunately, they entirely missed the potentially far more damaging charge linked to the testimony of the malleable Nelson Watkins, maker of the slung-shot. But then Watkins had already perjured himself by withholding information. If questioned by reporters, or by anyone, he would probably have held doggedly to his original story. Failing his own voluntary confession, no one could ever know that he—along with Charles Allen and who can tell how many others—saw Duff Armstrong use a weapon to strike James Metzger.

A final curious twist in the Armstrong story, centering on several campaign speeches by Lincoln, began some three months after the trial. Curious—but not at all clear as to purpose, even if deliberate, which itself is uncertain.

On the morning of August 12, 1857 Lincoln was back in Beardstown, coming upriver from Naples. This time he arrived in style, as befitted a candidate for the U.S. Senate, being greeted at the wharf by the blaring music of two bands and saluted by two volunteer military companies. Along State Street he was led to the National Hotel where he rested. That afternoon on an outdoor platform facing the river, in a two-hour speech he officially kicked off his campaign against Stephen Douglas. A block behind him as he spoke stood the courthouse that had so short a time before witnessed the legal drama he would never afterwards talk about. Beardstown was chosen for this event on grounds of strategy, it is said, allowing a prompt reply to Douglas. But how Lincoln really felt about the choice remains a question.

Continuing his campaign, Lincoln headed a few miles north to the town of Havana, site of the original Armstrong indictment and of the Norris conviction. There on August 14, a day after Douglas spoke, he gave another speech, which he opened with a humorous reference to a possible fistfight between himself and Douglas, "a pugilistic encounter." He declined the challenge, he said, getting a big laugh, because the question of which of them was the "more muscular" was not specified in the Republican platform. He also denied Douglas' charge that the Republicans were ganging up on him, that is, "playing *two upon one* against him" (Lincoln's italics), by having former senator Lyman Trumbull add his voice to the campaign. But, Lincoln went on, Douglas also had help, so "are not Douglas and this man playing *two upon one* against me? . . . And if it happens that there are two Democratic aspirants for Judge Trumbull's place, are they not playing *three upon one* against me, just as we are playing *two upon one* against him?" (all Lincoln's italics).

Decidedly, it was a peculiar note to sound in a speech made before people whose memory of the fatal, two-against-one attack on the unfortunate Metzger was still fresh. Was it simple coincidence? Could Lincoln have been oblivious to the local application of his little jibe? But if deliberate, to what purpose?

Two days later, just south of Havana at the town of Bath, Lincoln spoke again. Here he is heard making reference to his youthful days in Illinois, and to his old companions and neighbors and their sons. What he said was reported by the Chicago *Daily Press and Tribune*: "Among the old men, he had met more than half a dozen who were in the same company with him 27 years ago in the Black Hawk War . . . But what more reminded him of his advancing age, was the number of young men around him, now, and for years past, voters, who were the sons of his friends of early years, and are now the age he was when he first knew their fathers."

Quite natural, of course, that sentimental remark about the early days and the passage of years. No doubt it was prompted by his encountering those old comrades-in-arms, and perhaps by sad talk of the recent death of another old comrade from the Black Hawk War, stalwart Sergeant Jack Armstrong. Yet again, it seems downright peculiar, this pointed reference to the sons of his early friends, especially in view of what had happened to one of them at Beardstown shortly before. Behind it did there lay animated talk among the veterans about Lincoln's clever rescue of the dead Jack's son? Such talk, inevitably, would have focused on the now fast-spreading rumor about the faked almanac, to those old soldiers no doubt a slick dodge that brought nods of smiling approval, but something far else to Lincoln's political opponents.

In his final speech prior to the 1858 election, a brief one in late October, Lincoln openly complained that the raucous campaign had too often become ugly. He decried the way in which he'd been "bespattered with every imaginable odious epithet . . . I have culti-vated patience and made no attempt at a retort." Included in the slander thrown at him was the charge about the faked almanac. Lincoln lost that election, and studies of why and how he lost still continue. Whether stories about a deftly doctored almanac, circu-lated both in praise and blame, helped cause the loss no one today can tell.

APPENDICES

NOTES AND SOURCES

SELECTED BIBLIOGRAPHY

ACKNOWLEDGMENTS

THE WATKINS TESTIMONY AND
THE BRADY LETTER

I f it had not been for James Gridley's intense curiosity about the Armstrong case and trial, the revelations contained in the testimony of Nelson Watkins would never have been put on record. As it was, their survival involved a narrow escape indeed. Because of its unique importance in the story of the almanac trial, the Watkins evidence is given here in its entirety, verbatim from the Gridley article.

When in February 1909 Gridley began his researches, he consulted the old court papers at Beardstown (the first to do so), hunting primarily for a list of the Armstrong jurors. Some of the twelve, he hoped, would still be alive and willing to talk, not impossible even after the lapse of fifty years. Upon tracking down all twelve names he found that only two were then living: jury foreman Milton Logan, and John T. Brady. At age ninety, Logan was a resident of Boone, Iowa, three hundred miles west of Beardstown. Brady, whom Gridley recalled meeting during the Civil War in Beardstown, by then had long been living in Pomona, California.

Letters to both men brought no answer from Logan, who was

then in failing memory and who died just a year later. (Obit., *Journal of the Illinois Historical Society*, April 1910, 125). From Brady a reply soon arrived, starting a correspondence which quickly and dramatically realized Gridley's hopes of turning up new information. "He has written me at length of his recollections of the Armstrong trial," Gridley assured his readers, "and I have every confidence in the reliability of his information." From his own knowledge, Brady himself he styles "a retired capitalist, in the enjoyment of excellent health, and [with] his mental powers unimpaired . . . a man of much more than ordinary intelligence" (28). He doesn't give Brady's age at the time of the trial, but it was twenty-four (U.S. Census, Cass County, 1850), making him just seventy-five when he wrote his letter.

In his article Gridley proceeds in order: after presenting the facts of the crime, he gives the original indictment whole, and describes Lincoln's entry into the case. At this point he offers his initial quote from the Brady letter, not giving dates or other background. Totaling some seven hundred words, this section, much quoted from in my text, supplies nothing with relation to the Watkins charges.

Here Gridley interrupts the Brady letter to insert other material, then returns to Brady (whether quoting from the same letter as the first section, or another, he doesn't say, but he does allude to the "letters" received from Brady). Though he is about to publish to the world what amounts to a serious accusation against Lincoln's integrity as a lawyer, he introduces the passage very briefly and circumspectly, as if treating some incidental side issue. "The actual facts relative to the killing of Metzger," he writes, "are doubtless disclosed by these recitals." In that reticence, Gridley's hesitation, even embarrassment to a degree, are plainly evident, and well might be so, seeing what Brady wrote:

One of the witnesses in the Duff Armstrong case was Will Watkins, whose father lived near Petersburg in Menard

County. About two months after the Armstrong trial, T. B. Collins and myself were in the Watkins neighborhood buying cattle; Mr. Watkins sent his son Will with us, to help look up cattle. I recognized him as being the witness that Mr. Lincoln used to prove that Duff Armstrong did not have the slung-shot which was exhibited at the trial, in his possession. It naturally followed that we talked of the trial.

Will Watkins told me that Mr. Lincoln sent for him to come to Springfield; he questioned him about the slung-shot, and asked how it happened to be lost, and then found near the spot where Metzger was killed. He said he told Mr. Lincoln that when he laid down that night under the wagon to go to sleep, that he laid the slung-shot upon the reach of the wagon, and in the morning, forgot to get it, and when the wagon was driven away, it dropped off at the place where it was found.

Watkins said that he told Mr. Lincoln that he (Lincoln) did not want to use him (Watkins) as a witness, as he knew too much, and he began to tell Lincoln what he knew, and Mr. Lincoln would not allow him to tell him anything and said to Watkins: "All I want to know is this: Did you make that slung-shot? and did Duff Armstrong ever have it in his possession?" Watkins said he replied: "On cross-examination they may make me tell things I do not want to tell" and Mr. Lincoln assured him he would see to it that he was not questioned about anything but the slung-shot.

Watkins told me that Duff Armstrong killed Metzger by striking him in the eye with an old-fashioned wagon hammer and that he saw him do it. Watkins said that Douglas and all the other eight or ten witnesses for Armstrong who swore that Armstrong hit Metzger with his fist, all swore to a lie and they knew it, as they all knew he hit him with a wagon hammer.

During the trial Allen testified that Duff Armstrong hit Metzger with a slung-shot and I felt he was telling the truth until Mr. Lincoln proved by an almanac that Allen was so badly mistaken about it being a bright moonlit night: then Allen's whole testimony was discredited.*

In 1913 Gridley himself, following the death of his wife, moved to California, settling in Long Beach (thirty miles southwest of Pomona, where Brady lived). There, in his early seventies, he remarried, the bride being "an old schoolmate of his, Miss Emily Brady" (whether any relation of John Brady is not known; obit., *Journal of the Illinois Historical Society*, V. 19, 1926, 265–66). He died in 1924, leaving his second wife and seven children from his first marriage. About Brady himself nothing further is known.

An obvious question is *why* Brady kept silent for so many years about his revealing talk with Watkins. Just as obvious is the fact that the question cannot be answered, except to say that it is by no means certain that he did keep silent. He may in fact have told many people about it, no one believing him. Or perhaps he felt uncomfortable possessing such damning information about the martyred president and did stay quiet until approached by an inquirer from his hometown, someone he knew.

Whether Watkins actually said those precise things to Brady, made those exact statements, whether Brady correctly remembered what he'd been told, are questions that will occur to each reader. Personally, I am entirely satisfied that Watkins told only the truth about something in which he was directly concerned, and that Brady introduced no error or distortion. My principal reason for concluding so is easily stated: the Watkins testimony agrees with what is discoverable by other means as to Duff's guilt.

---

* *Journal of the Illinois Historical Society*, April 1910, 42–43. The name Will, in place of Nelson, may be a slip, or may be another of Watkins' names. In the article *slung-shot* appears as *sling-shot*, but I believe that Gridley has simply misread Brady's spelling, not understanding that *slung-shot* was correct.

Still another, and more intriguing but now unanswerable question concerns how much Lincoln actually knew, how much Watkins revealed to him that day in the Springfield office. If he told Lincoln everything he later told Brady—including the fact that "he saw" Duff deliver the fatal blow—then that day must have been among the most trying in Lincoln's life, committed as he was in heart and mind to Duff's defense.

THE ARMSTRONG JURY

Compiled from the U.S. Census 1850, 1860, and the Illinois State Census 1865, with additional information supplied by Mary A. Bell of Beardstown, and by Alice Schnake of the Beardstown Public Library. The basic source is the list of names in Gridley 28 which was copied from court documents now lost.

Name	Age	Occupation	Misc.
Milton Logan Beardstown, foreman	38	farmer	Died Boone, Iowa, Feb. 11, 1910. Buried Beardstown City Cemetery. Wife Margaret Bowen. Five children.
Horace Hill Husted Precinct	35–40	farmer	Died 1877, buried Karr Cemetery, Cass Co. Wife name Aurora (?). Three children.
Charles Marcy	30–40	not known	Served in Civil War, Co. B, 114th Ill. Vol. Inf. Married, two children.
George Seilschott Beardstown	32	merchant	Never married. Died April 19, 1862, buried Beardstown City Cemetery.

Benjamin Eyre Beardstown	24	Blacksmith	In Civil War, Co. E, 32nd Ill. Vol. Inf., killed in combat, Hatcher Run, Oct. 5, 1862. Wife Lydia, one dgtr.
John T. Brady Beardstown	24	business- man	Died Pomona, Cal., about 1915. The only juror to provide detailed comment on the trial. See Appendix A and the Index.
Samuel Neely Virginia, Ill.	28	not known	Beardstown trustee. In Va. served as postmaster 1855- 56. Wife named Kate.
John Johnson Beardstown	28	not known	In Civil War, Major, Co. B., 114th Ill. Vol. Inf. Married sec- ond time 1880, Morgan Co., Ill. Wives Mary & Elizabeth.
Nelson Graves	33	not known	Died Niantic, Macon Co., Ill. Dec. 6, 1896. Wife Eliza Jane Edgar.
Thornton Cole	not known	not known	No information. No listing in Census 1850, 1860, 1865 or any other source.
Matthew Armstrong	not known	not known	Died May 28, 1858, three weeks after the Armstrong trial. Wife Eliza Ann Lake.
Augustus Hoyer	30–40	not known	In Civil War, Lt., Co. B, 2nd Ill. Artillery. Buried Beardstown. Wife Marion Ewing.

NOTE: Two jurors (Hoyer and Marcy) show up in the 1865 state census but not in the 1860 U.S. Census. Three others not listed in 1860 (Johnson, Graves, Cole) probably left Cass County within two years of the trial. Aside from Gridley (see the Bibliography), there was no effort, at the time or later, to interview any of the twelve.

DUFF ARMSTRONG'S
STATEMENT

N ot until almost forty years had passed did the accused man agree to give an interview about the case for publication. When he did so, in the summer of 1896, interest in Lincoln biography was again intense, sparked by Ida Tarbell's series of articles in *McClure's* magazine. At his home in Ashland, not far from Beardstown, Duff was visited by a Springfield lawyer and sometime journalist, J. M. Davis, who did research for Tarbell. The resulting interview appeared in the New York *Sun*, Sunday, June 7, 1896, section 3, p. 2. The headline read: LINCOLN'S FAMOUS CASE, and a subhead announced DUFF ARMSTRONG'S STORY OF HIS OWN MURDER TRIAL. Some introductory comment by the *Sun's* editor is omitted here.

~⌒

It was on a Saturday night, and camp meeting was over for the day. In the edge of the grove were three bars where liquor was sold. Here gathered all the men and boys who went to camp meeting to drink whiskey and have a good time—and a great many went for no other purpose. I had been at the meeting two or three days, and had been drinking much, but I was then becoming sober. It was probably 10 o'clock when I found a big goods box not far from the bars, and I stretched myself out for a night's sleep.

Up to this time "Pres" Metzger and I had been good friends; but "Pres" had been drinking and was in an ugly mood. He came along making a great deal of noise, and said to me: "D—n you, get up." Then he grabbed my legs and pulled me off. In a few minutes he jerked me down again. I said, "Let me alone, Pres; I am sleepy." He went away but soon came back and pulled me off a third time, and took my hat, threw it upon the ground and stamped it. He said I had no business there; that I ought to be at home "picking up chips for my Ma."

I told him that was none of his business, and then I walked over to one of the long counters and called for a drink of whiskey. He followed and just as I lifted the glass to my lips he caught me by the throat, spilling the whiskey. I set down my glass and turned around and said to him: "Pres, if you do that again I will knock you down, [even] if you are bigger than I am; you have run this thing far enough."

He had a loaded whip in his hand and was determined to have a fight with me. I hit him a terrible blow, knocking the skin from one of my knuckles. We clinched and Pres rather got the best of me. I was strong for one of my size, and was able to catch him and throw him back over me. He got up first and came at me again. Then we fought like tigers. At last he got me under him. More than a hundred people stood by watching the fight and when the boys saw Pres was getting the best of me they pulled him off. We walked up to the bar, and each taking a drink of whiskey we bumped glasses and were friends again.

But Pres had not got through with me. As we stood there, without any warning he hit me a blow on the upper lip. He was going to hit me with a glass when another man said, "Set that down; if you strike him with that glass I will kill you." Then we parted. Metzger stole a quilt from a buggy nearby, and wrapping it around him walked off to bed. I saw nothing more of him until the next morning, when he walked up to the bar with the stolen quilt still around him. His right eye was swollen shut. He bathed it with a glass of whiskey, drank another glass, then mounted his horse and rode away. Several days after that he died. Then the officers came and arrested me and put me in jail.

I had a preliminary trial at Havana and was held without bail. All the bad luck in the world seemed to come to me now. On this very day my father, Jack Armstrong, died. On his deathbed he said to my mother, "Hannah, sell everything to clear Duff." These were almost his last words. I was a kind of favorite with my Ma and my Pa both. I always stayed at home with them.

After the change of venue to Beardstown, Lincoln told my mother he would defend me. At the trial I had about twenty-five witnesses. The strongest witness against me was Charles Allen. He was the witness that swore about the moon; he swore it was a full moon and almost overhead. Uncle Abe asked him about it over and over but he stuck to it. Then he said he saw me strike Metzger with a slung-shot. Uncle Abe asked him to tell how it was done. He got up and went through the motion, struck an overhand blow, just as he declared he saw me do by the light of the full moon. Uncle Abe had him do it over again.

After Allen's testimony everybody thought I would be

convicted. After Uncle Abe had talked to the jury a little while he said, "Now, I will show you that this man Allen's testimony is a pack of lies; that he never saw Armstrong strike Metzger with a slung-shot; that he did not witness this fight by the light of the full moon, for the moon was not in the heavens that night." And then Uncle Abe pulled out the almanac and showed the jury the truth about the moon.

I do not remember exactly what it was—whether the moon had not risen, or whether it had set; but whatever it was it upset Allen's story completely. He passed the almanac to the jurors and they all inspected it. Then Uncle Abe talked about the fight, and showed that I had acted in self-defense and had used no weapon of any kind. But it seemed to me Uncle Abe did his best talking when he told the jury what true friends my father and mother had been to him in the early days, when he was a poor young man at New Salem.

He told how he used to go out to Jack Armstrong's and stay for days; how kind mother was to him and how many a time he had rocked me to sleep in the old cradle. He said he was not there pleading for me because he was paid for it; but he was there to help a good woman who had helped him when he needed help. Lawyer Walker made a good speech for me too, but Uncle Abe's beat anything I ever heard.

As Uncle Abe finished his speech he said, "I hope this man will be a free man before sundown." The jury retired and nearly everybody went to supper. They left me there with the sheriff, [with] my brother Jim, and a parcel of the boys. The jury was in a room nearby, and it was not over five minutes after they went out when I heard them talking and laughing and my heart beat a little faster. As soon as the judge and the lawyers got back from supper the jury was brought in. They had to pass me and I eyed them closely for some hopeful sign. One of them looked at me and winked. Then I knew it was [all] right, and when the foreman handed up the verdict of "Not guilty" I was the happiest man in the world, I reckon.

Now my mother was not in the courtroom when the jury came in, and it is all stuff about her fainting and falling into my arms. She was away somewhere, I don't know just where. That night she went home with Jim Dick, the sheriff; I went home with Dick Overton, and as we went down the courthouse steps he slipped a five-dollar bill into my hand. Uncle Abe would not charge my mother a cent; he said her happiness over my freedom was his sufficient reward.

The almanac used by Lincoln was one which my cousin Jake Jones furnished him. On the morning of the trial I was taken outside the courtroom to talk to Lincoln. Jake Jones was with us. Lincoln said he wanted an almanac for 1857. Jake went right off and got one and brought it to Uncle Abe. It was an almanac for the proper year, and there was no fraud about it. The truth is, there was no moon that night; if there was, it was hidden by clouds. But it was light enough for everybody to see the fight. The fight took place in front of one of the bars, and each bar had two or three candles on it.

I had no slungshot; I never carried a weapon of any kind, never in my life. Metzger had a loaded whip, but he did not attempt to use it on me. It was only a fist fight, and if I killed Metzger I killed him with my naked fist.

James H. Norris was indicted with me for the killing of Metzger. He was tried at Havana before my trial was had. Now, he had no more to do with the fight than any of the other bystanders; but he had killed a man some time before, and had gotten clear, and everybody seemed to think this would be a good chance to give him his just deserts. So they sent him to the penitentiary for eight years.

When the war broke out the four brothers of us enlisted in the army. Jim was wounded at Belmont; Pleasant died. I served on until the end of the war, when mother took a notion she wanted me. People laughed at her when she said she would write to the President, but she said, "Please goodness, I am a-going to try it." She got Squire Garber of Petersburg to write to Uncle Abe, and in a few days mother got a telegram signed "A. Lincoln" telling her I had been honorably discharged. At that time I was at Elmira, N.Y., helping pick up deserters, and a discharge was the last thing I was thinking of.

Especially interesting and revealing is Armstrong's confusion and indecision about the lighting of the fight scene. He can't say anything about the moon at the critical moment except that it gave no light (he is the only one to mention clouds). Even so, he insists, the bystanders could see the fight by the light of the candles on the bar. The difficulty arose because of his need for concealment: his personal, initial encounter with Metzger he emphasizes while leaving room for Lincoln's almanac strategy, which refers to the later, unmentioned attack by himself and Norris. Of course by the time of the interview no one remained who could tell the difference.

The details he gives about his admitted fight with Metzger may be taken as more or less accurate. But of course he denies using a weapon, then or later, during his subsequent fatal attack on Metzger in concert with Norris. In fact, Norris himself is not mentioned at all until near the close of the interview, and a casual reader would hardly have understood how the second man fitted into the picture.

What Duff says about his cousin Jake supplying Lincoln with an almanac the morning of the trial is an obvious error. Lincoln would certainly have brought with him the needed volume for his planned attack on Charles Allen's testimony about the moon. The cousin, it may be, on his own went looking for another copy. The details he gives about Lincoln's questioning of the witness Allen are also not quite accurate, especially where he has Lincoln telegraphing his strategy.

Duff is wrong again (this time it seems on purpose) when he says that his discharge from the army during the Civil War came while he was in New York State rounding up deserters. Actually his discharge, personally ordered by Lincoln at the earnest request of his mother Hannah Armstrong, came while Duff was a patient in an army hospital at Louisville, Kentucky (see above, 102). The year before, he had himself been listed as a deserter, returning to his unit only when a general amnesty was declared. He was later denied a military pension because of the lapse, as was his wife after his death.

NOTES AND SOURCES

In addition to the usual source citations, included here is a full discussion of every significant point—and many more ephemeral—in the foregoing narrative. Mingled with these discussions is much additional information which may be of interest or value.

Citations of the original court documents refer to copies in my possession, kindly supplied by the Lincoln Legals, Springfield. The originals themselves are preserved at the Cass County seat, Virginia, some also being filed at the court of original jurisdiction, Havana, Mason County.

Citations of published sources are given in shortened form and may be identified by a glance at the Bibliography.

For the citation *Informants* see the bibliography under Wilson and Davis. The left-hand margin displays *page* numbers.

Prologue: Not Too Late

2   *Death of Jack Armstrong*: No official record of the date or cause has been found. Hannah said it took place in 1857 but gave no month or day. Duff later placed his father's passing on "the very day" that the Metzger indictment was handed down at Havana, which was November 5, 1857. A search of available newspapers has turned up no obituary.

2   "The framework of his"—Herndon 270. Davis' remarks, says Herndon, were delivered two months after Lincoln's death in a eulogy at Indianapolis. Herndon adds his own full agreement, making the sentiment unanimous with the two who knew Lincoln as a lawyer best: "Two things were essential to his success in managing a case. One was time; the other a feeling of confidence in the justice of the cause he represented" (Herndon 272). With neither Davis nor Herndon, so far as is known, did Lincoln ever

talk about his work in the Armstrong case—no accident, in the opinion of this writer.

3   "the moon had already"—Donald 151. In his note to this statement (622), Donald strangely contradicts himself. Remarking on the fake almanac charge, he says Lincoln would have had no need for a fake because "at the time of the murder the moon was very low and near to setting." He adds that the truth about the moon's position has "recently" been settled, where it was actually established beyond doubt a century ago (see Lamon 329 and Gridley 27). Another slip in the Donald text is his description of the witness Allen saying that the moon was "directly overhead." What Allen really said was that the moon was *almost* directly overhead, a difference emphasized at the trial.

This curious fumbling with the facts regarding the moon can be seen in much of the incidental writing on the case. In a book otherwise excellent, *Lincoln as a Lawyer*, the author, John Frank, gives a two-page description of the case. At one point he says that Lincoln trapped a witness as to the exact position of the *risen* moon "with an almanac which showed that the moon was not at the time where the witness said it was." (176). But a page later he again alludes to the moon, this time saying it had *set*: "genuine almanacs for the year in question show that the moon was not out at the time the witness said it was" (177, Frank's italics).

Just as culpable were the earlier, full-length biographies of Lincoln. Isaac Arnold (1865, p. 88) blandly states that at the time of the fight there was "no moon at all," a claim echoed by Noah Brooks (1888, p. 128), Lord Charnwood (1916, p. 106), and Ida Tarbell (1925, II, 67). Carl Sandburg confusedly notes that the moon had set just before midnight "which raised a question whether there was enough light" for somebody to see by an hour before (1926, p. 126). Benjamin Thomas gets it nearly right but then stumbles into a contradiction: "The moon had almost set and the night was dark" (1952, p. 159). Stephen Oates correctly states that the moon "was low in the sky about an hour away from setting," but then misses the significance of a low-lying moon (1977, p. 141). I should add that much of the confusion, early and late, stems from uncritical reliance on an inept comment made by Lincoln's assistant counsel in the case, William Walker. See below, 145.

I make these comments not to point a finger at anyone, but to demonstrate how highly competent professionals tend, even now, to confuse and misstate the facts of the Armstrong case, largely because it has never been adequately investigated or reported.

4   *the original trial records.* These include some seventy separate handwritten documents, totaling nearly 150 pages. Many record simple clerical actions, for instance docket notations, witness travel vouchers, and a variety of subpoenas. But also present are some more significant items such as the grand jury indictment, the judge's charge to the jury, and a brief "transcript" of the Norris trial.

4   *J. N. Gridley:* As he states, it was his hearing the tales of a supposedly fraudulent almanac used by Lincoln that got him started, "being absolutely unable to believe that Abraham Lincoln would be guilty of such outrageous conduct" (26). To aid his search there was then almost nothing reliable in print (1909), though he did have, as he says, an unpublished paper by a member of the Beardstown Ladies Club, "Mrs. Dr. Schweer." (For further on Gridley's search see Appendix A.) By profession a lawyer, Gridley wrote several other historical articles, as well as a history of Cass County. He died in California in 1924 (obit, *Journal of Illinois State Historical Society,* V. 19, 265).

Despite its defects and obvious lacunae, as a pioneer effort by an enthusiastic amateur, Gridley's article was well done. For one thing, it first uncovered the crucial Nelson Watkins testimony when Gridley began correspondence with the juror Brady. Only with this element in place does the Armstrong case and trial begin at last to make sense.

5   "who professes personal"—Barrett 63. The name of the author is not given, and I suspect that the whole distorted account was lifted by Barrett from an earlier magazine article. Judge Harriott in his 1866 interview with Herndon may have been referring to this article when he said of some unidentified magazine piece about the trial that it was "from beginning to end a humbug" (*Informants* 703). Part of the "humbug" aspect is seen in the article's exaggerated claim that the case attracted great public attention: ". . . a feverish desire for vengence seized upon the infatuated populace while only prison bars prevented a horrible death at the hands of a mob. The events were heralded in the newspapers, painted in the highest colors" (Barrett 63). In reality there was no detailed or continuing coverage of either of the two trials. The *Illinois State Journal* on November 19, 1857, for instance, gave the outcome of the Norris trial only a dozen lines,

saying that Norris had been sentenced to eight years in the penitentiary, and that Armstrong had been granted a change of venue.

5   "had for months been"—Barrett 65. The witness in question was Charles Allen, whose testimony about the moon Lincoln so cleverly impugned. While it is true that Allen on the stand was laughed at by the spectators, he didn't leave the courtroom, staggering or otherwise, but returned to his seat. Also, as my text makes clear, Allen was not a perjurer, only in one point mistaken. For further discussion see below, 145.

6   *The film* Young Mr. Lincoln: Admittedly, in cinematic terms the movie's dealing fast and loose with the true facts of the case, as then understood, is effective. Yet how much more compelling— far deeper in suggestiveness and infinitely more dramatic in its revelation of the complications inherent in human motive— would have been the reality, could it have been known! Of course when *Young Mr. Lincoln* was made, sixty years ago, it would not have been possible even to suggest the full truth about Lincoln's deliberate manipulation of the evidence.

Chapter One: Killing at Walker's Grove

11   *Death of James Metzger*: The primary source is the grand jury indictment, given at Havana, November 5, 1857. Also statements by the attorneys Walker and Shaw (*Informants* 22, 316, and Gridley 30). My picture of the injured man arriving home the night of the fight is obvious in the circumstances of the case.

13   *The crime*: Grand jury indictment, November 5, 1857; Norris trial transcript; testimony of attorneys Walker and Shaw (*Informants* 316, 332, Gridley 25, 30, 43).

16   *Trial of Norris*: Transcript; motion to quash; motion for arrest of judgment; Attorneys Walker and Shaw (*Informants* 22–23, 316), Gridley 34. Norris' previous indictment on a murder charge, actually manslaughter, involving a man named Thornburg, was first mentioned in Gridley 34. Aside from a successful plea of self-defense, nothing further was supplied, not even as to a date. In later writings the fact itself is often mentioned but no additional information has surfaced. Today at the courthouse in Havana no records of the charge or the trial are to be found, but a family by the name of Thornburg did reside in Havana at the time. According to a mention in a Mason County history, two of the Thorn-

burg sons died young, Mahlon in 1852, and Jonathan in 1854 (*History of Menard and Mason counties*, Baskin & Co., Chicago, 1879, p. 263). Whether either of these had a connection with Norris cannot at the moment be determined. If the Thornburg action came up in any manner during the Metzger proceedings, the surviving documents do not reflect it.

16 *Armstrong change of venue*: From the original document, dated November 5, 1857. Whether among the people of Mason County there really was some "prejudice against" Armstrong is undocumented. It is possible, even probable, that there did exist some public sentiment over Metzger's death, especially because of its brutal manner. Gridley without offering proof mentions in passing "the great excitement of the people over the affair" (30), and says that because the jailhouse at Havana was insecure the prisoners were taken across the river to the Lewiston jail in Fulton County. But if there was bad feeling toward Armstrong, what about Norris? Why didn't he too apply for a change of venue?

17 *Conviction of Norris*: The written verdict, bearing the signatures of all twelve jurors, survives: "We the jury agree to find the defendant guilty of manslaughter & as penalty eight years service in the State penitentiary." The signers: John Davis, Isaiah Williams, E. P. Lapham, Robert Anderson, H. W. Kent, Jacob Stease, I. Patton, William Hartzell, C. Riggs, L. S. Jonas, Isaac Ware, E. B. Sweet. The five prosecution witnesses are named in surviving travel vouchers and subpoenas. Promptly after conviction, the lawyers, Dilworth and Campbell, moved for an "Arrest of Judgment," and a new trial. Their reasons were several, among them questioning the form of the indictment, asserting that the evidence was inadequate, and challenging the propriety of the charge to the jury. The motion was disallowed.

17 *Distance of witnesses from the scene of the crime*: Strangely, none of the surviving court documents specify this crucial statistic. Only in the jury instructions given by the judge at the Norris trial is the topic mentioned at all: "The jury may take into consideration the distance Allen was from the parties, to wit, Armstrong & Norris, the time of night, the distance the witness was from Metzger . . ." The mention proves at least that the distance *was* a point of contention (apparently as part of a defense effort to prove mistaken identity). Norris' conviction, however, amply demonstrates that the defense failed to make significant any argument as to distance, so that the jury was not troubled by doubts on that score.

About the distance the lawyer Walker some seven years afterward supplied differing estimates. First he cited a figure of thirty or forty feet ("10 or 15 paces," *Informants* 22). A year after that he thought it was about ninety feet ("30 yards distant," *Informants* 325). In the subsequent literature on the case all statements about distance are no more than casual estimates. Some rise blithely as high as 150 feet, half the length of a football field! I am satisfied that the actual distance of the witnesses from the fight was well under fifty feet (see above, 58-60, for a discussion). A related question about Allen being at all near the scene when the crime took place also came up at the Norris trial. It was charged that he had gone elsewhere in the campground. But this point, too, was quickly eliminated, judging by the jury instructions.

18   *Dying request of Jack Armstrong*: Duff later recalled hearing from his mother that his father, almost with his final breath, urged her to do whatever was necessary to save their son, including selling the farm: "Hannah, sell everything to clear Duff. These were almost his last words." (Interview, see *Appendix C*, 123). That Jack personally suggested approaching Lincoln is my own conclusion.

Chapter Two: Send for Abe Lincoln

21   *The Douglas threat*: This quite remarkable development in Lincoln's political life by now is a familiar part of his story: see any full-length biography, for instance, Donald 202–205, Luthin 191–96, or Fehrenbacher, *Prelude* 133–37. Throughout the months of his preparation for and conduct of the Armstrong case, Lincoln was kept constantly on edge by Douglas' adroit twists and turns in the volatile situation.

22   *Lincoln visited by Edwards*: See Fehrenbacher, *Recollected* 149–50, which quotes an 1860 interview with Edwards, giving Lincoln's words as in my text. An editorial note explains that Edwards' memory of the event "does not agree with that of Armstrong's wife, Hannah," meaning that Hannah claimed to have herself written to Lincoln which is true (Informants 526). But the interview in which Edwards made his claim took place only three years after the fact, and Hannah, who was illiterate, would have needed help with her letter, even in knowing just where and how to send it. The obvious answer is as I give it. She used the willing Edwards, an old friend of both parties, if not to write the letter

for her, at least to carry it to Springfield—of course, a common practice at that time among people who wanted to be sure a letter would reach its destination.

Edwards and Lincoln had been very well acquainted, the two having shared some business transactions years before. That they were still well acquainted in 1858 is seen in a letter Edwards wrote Lincoln while he was president-elect and waiting in Springfield to start his journey to Washington. Edwards writes to say that because Lincoln is now the center of so much attention, he won't be visiting: "If I was to travel through the cold to Springfield, I could have no satisfaction with you, for you are surrounded continually by a class of mind that cares for nothing but office, and would sacrifice you or Jesus or anybody else, and what few honest men there is left in the land has to stand back" (Mearns II, 397). He also reminds Lincoln of a meeting they had on January 30, 1860, when Edwards, he says, predicted that Lincoln would get the presidential nomination.

The question of a fee for Lincoln came up a second time when Hannah, at the close of the trial in Beardstown, asked about it. Again Lincoln refused, saying emphatically that "anything I can do for you I will do willingly and freely without charge" (*Informants* 526). This assurance is perhaps what led her five years later to ask President Lincoln to discharge Duff, then ill with rheumatism, from the army (see p. 157, below).

24   *The wrestling match*: Several later sources recall this event, some of them eyewitnesses. Most of the eyewitnesses can be found in *Informants*: 73–74 (James Short), 80 (Nult Green, brother of William), 369 (Henry McHenry), 386 (Robert Rutledge), 402 (John Rutledge), 528 (Henry Clark); see also Mearns I, 154, 159 (William Green and Royal Clary); also Basler 394, 399, and Wilson 20, 326 (Stuart). While none of these gives a complete or detailed description of the bout's progress and outcome, close analysis along with a grasp of the sport permits a fairly reliable reconstruction. Beyond all the technical details of holds, falls, etc., what mattered was the final, quite unexpected result, how it brought the young battler immediate acceptance, even leadership, among the Clary's Grove bunch.

A more recent (1998) and rather unusual study of the match is offered by Douglas Wilson (*Honor's Voice* 20–51). Certainly the lengthiest treatment yet attempted of the colorful event, Wilson recognizes that his approach may seem like overkill (at thirty-

plus pages, it's a legitimate fear!). Accordingly, he opens by deliberately stressing its fitness for full-scale historical inquiry. Because
of Lincoln's later status in the nation's pantheon, he writes, the
match is lifted "from a rowdy initiation rite in an obscure pioneer
village into a notable historical event" (21). However, Wilson
proves to be not so much interested in the match itself as a sport-
ing event as he is in refuting the best-known fact connected with
it: Lincoln's own later claim that it was a—or *the*—"turning
point" in his young life. Wilson's marshaling and minute analysis
of the evidence, his weaving of his interpretations with the details
of Lincoln's political life, is a virtuoso performance. Before he fin-
ishes, the wrestling match has come to seem indeed a "notable"
event, well beyond anything that an ordinary view of such things
could have expected.

But of course there's the rub. In the overall, except to Lincoln
personally at the moment, that fleeting, long-ago tussle in the
dust at New Salem *wasn't* important. It was *only* a wrestling
match, and will remain so. In spite of Wilson's clever juggling, it
can't be made to serve any higher purpose, not a pennyworth
more than what it meant in the life of the young Lincoln. In fact,
in trying to raise it to a higher level Wilson has fallen into one of
the more subtle errors in historical inquiry, building lofty theo-
ries on inadequate sources. For this particular wrestling match
the sources are so skimpy and offhand—were never *meant* to be
anything more—that they can bear the weight of only so much
analytical pressure, far less than Wilson imposes.

As a wrestler Lincoln remained unbeaten for only another
year after his New Salem bout. In camp during the Black Hawk
War he encountered his first loss, in fact was for the first time
actually thrown. Interestingly, the details of the defeat curiously
mirror what happened with Armstrong. The match was against a
sergeant from another militia company, an experienced wrestler
named Lorenzo Dow Thompson (apparently named for a famous
frontier preacher of the time, Lorenzo Dow). In a titanic struggle
that was deafeningly cheered by men from both companies,
Thompson clearly won the first fall, throwing Lincoln flat. The
second fall, in which both men went down, seemed to Lincoln's
men to be a "dog fall," a draw. But Thompson's followers roared
back that it had been a "fair fall," and that therefore their man had
won, taking the necessary two out of three falls. Things quickly
got ugly—large sums had been bet on the outcome—and for

some moments a riot seemed in prospect. This Lincoln brought
to a halt by declaring that the fall had been a fair one, and
Thompson was the victor. Years later when questioned about the
match, he again admitted his defeat, adding that the burly
Thompson "could have thrown a grizzly bear" (*Magazine of History*, Tarrytown, N.Y., No. 77, 1921, 43–46; see also Fehrenbacher,
Recollected 332–33).

29   *Hannah's visit to Lincoln*: In her later statement she says that
she wrote Lincoln about her son, and when he responded, also
by letter, she "went to see Lincoln at Springfield—Saw him in
his office." (*Informants* 525–26). Elsewhere in her statement she
says that her first visit to Springfield was in 1859, an obvious
error, hers or the interviewer's. She adds that after Lincoln's
election as president she went again to Springfield to bid him
goodbye.

Some older treatments of the case quote a supposed letter
from Lincoln to Hannah in which he volunteers his services on
behalf of Duff, initiating the contact (for instance, Woldman
11–12). An obvious forgery, the letter first came to light in a 1909
booklet, *Footprints of Abraham Lincoln*, edited by the Rev. J. T.
Dobson. Variously reprinted, it gained some undeserved
respectability, being accepted by some writers who should have
known better.

29   *Lincoln as a criminal lawyer*: For information on this topic, a fairly
new one for which the needed material is only now becoming
available, I am indebted to the Lincoln Legals Project, Springfield;
see for instance its *Lincoln Legal Briefs*, No. 39, 1996. Also helpful
were the books by Duff, Woldman, and Frank. After the Armstrong affair, Lincoln handled only two other murders, winning
one and losing one. That of Peachy Harrison, tried in the summer
of 1859, in some ways was curiously similar to that of Armstrong.
It involved the grandson of Lincoln's old political adversary, Peter
Cartwright, the defendant being clearly guilty of stabbing an
acquaintance to death. By emphasizing the emotional aspects of
the case, and rather fiercely attacking a particular ruling of the
presiding judge, Lincoln won an acquittal (Duff 363–64, Woldman 108–110, Donald 150, Luthin 169).

30   "with the tacit approval"—East 79. This article gives a full
description of the Goings case, pointing up Lincoln's part in the
old lady's escape. Interestingly, the prosecutor and the judge were
the same two men as for the Armstrong trial, Fullerton and Har-

riott—making more understandable their apprehension about unexpected moves when Lincoln showed up at Beardstown.

30   *The Anderson murder case*: Information from the Lincoln Legals Project, Springfield; also Duff 330–31.

31   *Lincoln's preparation for the Armstrong trial*: This is nowhere exactly described in the literature (mostly because of the myth that he didn't do much!). But that it consumed an intense ten-day period, then with the continuance of the trial went on during another six months, becomes clear in the light of existing evidence. A local tradition that Lincoln inspected the crime scene, taking measurements and making a diagram, is in Lucas. Previous writers all state that for the details of the Norris trial Lincoln had to rely only on the personal notes of the attorney Walker. Actually he had in addition copies of certain documents supplied to the Beardstown court by the prosecutor at Havana (correspondence between James Taylor, clerk, Cass County Circuit Court and R. Ritter, clerk, Mason County Circuit Court). Included was a supposed "transcript" of the Norris trial (very brief and undetailed, a description rather than a record of the trial). Lincoln's information about what was said at the Havana trial about the moon must have come from Walker, his notes, and in conversation, probably also from talks with some of the witnesses.

32   *Guilt of Duff Armstrong*: To now, the question of Armstrong's guilt or innocence has never been adequately addressed, the latter being generally assumed because of the jury verdict. Some of the specific testimony is now lost, for instance the details of what was said by the prosecution witnesses. But what remains is more than enough to make it morally certain that Duff *did* hit Metzger in the face with the murderous slung-shot, a crushing blow, perhaps more than one. That alone makes him at least equally guilty of the man's death with the convicted Norris. Henry Shaw, who assisted the prosecutor and was a friend and admirer of Lincoln, never altered his belief concerning the guilt of "that criminal" Armstrong. He was sure that Armstrong had not been cleared "by any want of testimony against him" but by the skill of Lincoln in his defense (*Informants* 333, 316). The testimony of Nelson Watkins, if it had not been suppressed by Lincoln, when taken with that of Allen and the other witnesses would certainly have resulted in a conviction.

A significant addition to the question is rather unwittingly made by the biographer William Barton. For his account of the trial, Barton interviewed many of the Armstrong's old neighbors in Menard County, including some who had attended the trial. Duff by then had been dead only a few years, and Barton, as he reported, found a settled, surprisingly widespread belief in his guilt, a conviction that Lincoln "as a reward for Hannah Armstrong's kindness to him when he was a poor boy, had cleared a guilty man." The disconcerted Barton conciously reported the finding but managed to downplay it by dropping it into the midst of a lengthy footnote (Barton 316). The local belief in Duff's guilt, and in Lincoln's full awareness of it, is supported by Allen Lucas, earlier a prominent Beardstown lawyer and politician. See Bibliography.

34   *Testimony of Nelson Watkins*: Though not written down until many years later, the Watkins statements come from an especially strong source, the juror John Brady—according to Gridley, who knew him well, "a man of much more than ordinary intelligence" (Gridley 28). Some two months after the trial, Brady met Watkins at his home and they talked freely, with Watkins describing exactly what happened when he went to see Lincoln in Springfield. Brady's letter to Gridley (43–45) gives it all plainly and in detail (see Appendix A). Why this material was not picked up and used long ago I will not attempt to explain. The few writers who mention it at all do so in some embarrassment. The article by Wheeler affords a good example. It does allude to Watkins and his damning statements, but so confusedly, and without giving any source, that the charges are robbed of all impact. Other writers who show an acquaintance with the Gridley article manage altogether to ignore the Watkins material in it (see Townsend, Hodges, etc.). Even the valuable *Lincoln Encyclopedia* (Neely) while listing Gridley as a source, says only that "Lincoln produced a witness" who claimed he had the slung-shot "in his possession the night of the brawl" (p. 8). The rest of Watkins' stark testimony is simply ignored. Gridley himself shies away from the evidence he'd turned up, referring the reader for "the actual facts" to the Watkins' statements in the Brady letter which he quotes in full (42).

That it was Lincoln who initiated the contact with Watkins, an important point, is clear from his admission that "Lincoln sent for me" (Gridley 42). Brady's meeting with Watkins happened, as he says, entirely by accident: being in the neighborhood to buy cattle he visited the Watkins farm where he met and recognized

Watkins and "it naturally followed that we talked of the trial"
(Gridley 42). The original of the Brady letter has not been found.
Probably it was taken to California (Long Beach) when Gridley
moved there in 1913 and where he died in 1924.

No doubt some will object that the Watkins evidence as given
in the Brady letter is neither first-hand nor contemporary. That is
true, of course, and must be seriously considered (the claimed
conversation *was* contemporary, though its writing down apparently was not). Yet its provenance is solid, reported by a responsible party who had himself been directly involved in the trial, and
who had received the information first-hand from the witness
himself. Further, it fits easily into what is known about the crime
otherwise. Unpleasant as it may be in its implications, indeed in
its overt accusations, it is time to look the Watkins charge against
Lincoln straight in the eye.

34	"he knew too much"—Gridley 42.
34	"Did you make that"—Gridley 42.
35	"would not allow"—Gridley 42.
35	"he questioned him about"—Gridley 42.
36	"They may make me tell"—Gridley 42. Same for the next quota-tion in this paragraph.
37	"Saw him do it"—Gridley 42.
37	"They all swore to"—Gridley 42. Concerning Watkins' claim that the weapon Duff used on Metzger was what he called a "wagon hammer," I suggest that here Watkins himself was lying. Perhaps understandably, he feared having the slung-shot, made by him and brought by him to the campground that night, implicate him in the crime. This is aside from the fact that his story about leav-ing the slung-shot under a wagon forced him to specify a differ-ent weapon used by Duff. Between the two assertions obviously there are cross-purposes, which I have not yet untangled: which came first, the claim about the weapon being a wagon hammer, or the claim about the loss of the slung-shot?

For what it is worth, the U.S. Census for 1860 (Menard
County) seems to reveal some sort of closeness between the
Watkins and Armstrong families. Nelson Watkins is listed, with
five other children, as part of a household under a widow,
Lucinda Watkins, aged fifty-one. Two entries before this there
occurs the household of Isaac Watkins, which includes two Armstrongs, Robert and his wife Eliza. The closeness in the census
listing (numbers 603 and 605, sheet 86), suggests a relationship

because the entries are given in "the order of visitation." The two Watkins families, in other words, resided in close proximity to each other. One of Duff's five brothers was named Robert, but whether this is he cannot now be determined. It's true, of course, that the Armstrongs were a widespread clan in Menard and Mason and surrounding counties. Not all of these were related, a fact pretty well proved by the presence on the Armstrong jury of a certain Matthew Armstrong (Gridley 28).

37   "About where the sun"—Gridley 40, in Brady's letter. By others it is stated that Allen gave the moon's position as where the sun would be "about ten o'clock in the morning." (For instance, Shaw in *Informants* 316.) But this is surely a slip of memory, for the sun at about ten A.M. describes a rising moon, well short of the meridian. Such a position could hardly have been confused with the established fact that at eleven P.M. on the night of the fight the setting moon was well down on the horizon.

38   *Trial continuance to spring*: The unexpected fact that it was the prosecution that asked for the delay, and not Lincoln, is clear in the original court document: "And now on this day come the People of the State of Illinois, by their attorney, Hugh Fullerton, Esquire . . . whereupon a motion was made on the part of the People for a continuance until the next term of this court, which after due deliberation by the court was granted" (Gridley 38; the document apparently is no longer extant). At the same session a request that Duff be released on bail was denied.

38   "at the critical point"—Bergen 391. Lincoln's reputation among opposing lawyers for sudden strategic swerves during a trial was well described by Herndon, who watched or took part in many of them: "That which Lincoln's adversaries in a law suit feared most of all was his apparent disregard of custom or professional propriety in managing a case before a jury. He brushed aside all rules, and very often resorted to some strange and strategic performance which invariably broke his opponent down or exercised some peculiar influence over the jury. Hence the other side of the case were in constant fear of one of his dramatic strokes, or trembled lest he should 'ring in' some ingeniously planned interruption not on the programme" (Herndon 288).

Of course, this aspect of Lincoln's involvement is tied in with his effort from the first to keep his involvement secret, or as quiet and uncertain as might be possible (see below for further discussion, 142).

Chapter Three: In the Courtroom

41   *Lincoln's arrival at Beardstown*: Prior writings on the case all give
        this date as May 6, the day before the trial began, agreeing with
        the legend that Lincoln had only a single night to prepare. I
        believe he would never have cut it that close, but was in Beards-
        town by Sunday, May 2, not waiting in Danville for the end of
        the court term on May fifth. He was definitely in Danville on Sat-
        urday, May 1, when he gave a receipt for a legal fee (Angle 226).
        On May 3–5 in the Danville court he did have cases called but
        these could have been handled by his circuit court partner (infor-
        mation from the Lincoln Legals Project, Springfield, my gratitude
        to Martha Benner). First to state a May 6 arrival, though without
        proof, was Gridley 39. This was repeated by Barton who has him
        arriving in Beardstown "on the night before the trial," not naming
        a source (311), and that date has been accepted ever since.

        A related consideration is Lincoln's participation in two other
        court cases at this same spring term in Beardstown. In one, a
        holdover from the fall term, his help had been asked by the attor-
        ney Henry Shaw. In the other, involving a Springfield client of
        Lincoln's, Shaw was the opposing counsel. (See Shaw in *Infor-
        mants* 332–33.) Neither case required much preparation by Lin-
        coln, but both add support for the claim that he would have been
        on hand in Beardstown well before the sixth.

        One remark of Shaw's with respect to these two extra cases
        bears on still another aspect of Lincoln's connection with the
        Armstrong affair, that he wished to keep advance news about his
        participation as quiet as possible for as long as possible. Shaw, on
        his own word, actually didn't know until almost the last moment
        that in the Armstrong trial he would have Lincoln opposing him:
        "At the May term I expected Mr. Lincoln down to assist in the
        alimony case again, & he came in due time . . . I still thought that
        Mr. Lincoln had come to our court more particularly to attend to
        the Gill & Moore cases, and was very much surprised afterwards
        to see the immense interest he took in the Armstrong case"
        (*Informants* 333). Since Lincoln's work on the Armstrong defense
        had begun six months before, and he was at Beardstown the pre-
        vious fall when the court granted a continuance, it must have cost
        him some effort to so obscure his link with the case that opposing
        counsel remained unaware of it.

42   *Witness list, defense*: compiled from the original subpoenas and travel vouchers, Cass and Mason county courts. How many of the twenty-two were eyewitnesses, how many were put on the stand, is not certain. The juror Brady recalled the number of defense witnesses who actually testified as "eight or ten" (Gridley 40, 42).

42   *Witness list, prosecution*: compiled from the original subpoenas and travel vouchers, Cass and Mason county courts. Whether the dozen were all eyewitnesses to the crime isn't certain, though very probable. Their names: Charles Allen, Joseph Douglas, William Douglas, William Haines, Andrew Killion, A. P. Killion, William Killion, Grigsby Metzger, William Powers, Hamilton Rogers, Joseph Spelts, James Walker. The fourth name in that list, William Haines of Havana, comes up again in connection with the pardon request of James Norris (see chapter four). Why Haines, evidently a friend of Norris, should have appeared as a witness against Duff Armstrong, I cannot explain. The original subpoena clearly states he is being called to give evidence "in behalf of the People," of course meaning the prosecution.

    Of the three Killion brothers, at least one took the stand, for Lincoln in questioning William asked if he was the son of "old Jake Killion," whom Lincoln had known in earlier years. The reply was yes, and Lincoln commented, "Well, if you take after your dad you're a smart boy." The incident was recalled for Ida Tarbell about 1890 by another of the prosecution witnesses, William Douglas (Tarbell 278).

42   *Dr. Charles Parker*: The subpoena calling for him to testify on behalf of the defendant was not issued until the day before the trial. But of course he and Lincoln had been in close touch well before that. Strangely, Parker's testimony gets no mention in Lamon, Bergen, Gridley, or Barton, or any of the other early accounts. Only in Beveridge (566–67) is his crucial role finally explained and understood. Later it was insisted by Judge Harriott that Parker's session on the stand was the real key to the defense, of much more weight than the "moon theory" in winning an acquittal: "The almanac may have cut a figure, but it was Doct. Parkers testimony confirming Lincoln's theory—the Court saw this" (*Informants* 704).

42   *Duff Armstrong illiterate*: Like many of his friends among the defense witnesses who signed their travel vouchers with an X, Duff as late as 1884 similarly marked his army pension papers (Hannah Armstrong Materials, Lincoln Public Library, Springfield). The statement in Gridley 39 that Duff learned to read dur-

ing his six months in the Beardstown jail awaiting trial may or may not be true. But he never learned to write. A signature supposedly written by him, using his real first name, William, is on the application for a change of venue from Havana. But the handwriting is the same as that in the body of the document, where the name again occurs, the hand exactly mirroring the signature at the close. The lawyer or clerk who prepared the document apparently was not aware that Duff couldn't even sign his name. His mother was also illiterate, his father probably not. Several surviving documents from New Salem, where Jack served for a time as a constable, bear his signature (The Lincoln Library, Fort Wayne).

44   *Attempt to prevent Charles Allen's testimony*: First stated by Gridley 25, 39, relying in part on an interview with Duff's brother, Asbury, by Mrs. Schweer (see also Barton 316). The initial subpoena for Allen was issued with many others on April 23, 1858. The second subpoena, calling on the sheriff to produce Allen "instanter," is dated May 5, 1858, and the special writ issued to all sheriffs came the next day. Various reasons for Allen's absenting himself have been suggested. But the evidence all points to the situation I describe.

44   *Jury selection*: While no actual record of the process survives, it is obvious that the defense would prefer younger men and the prosecution older. The only listing of their names is found in Gridley 28, taken from a document no longer to be found. For the names along with as much information on each of the twelve men as can now be recovered, see my Appendix B. Aside from Brady, and to an extent Logan, none of them left anything personal on record about the trial, nor do any of their names appear elsewhere in the story. The statement by one writer on the case that Lincoln "succeeded in getting a jury of young men, the average age being less than thirty years" (Duff 354) rests on tradition but is supported by fact: see Appendix B.

44   *Henry Shaw*: A lengthy biographical sketch is in Perrin 260–65. After suffering a stroke in 1873 he gave up the law and entered the state legislature. He died in 1885, aged sixty.

45   "The lowest part of"—Bergen 390. This picture of Lincoln staring at the ceiling before the trial began is often misquoted as depicting his manner during the trial, which is far different from his usual alert attitude. His strategy at Beardstown, it seems, did include his sitting by at times and allowing his co-counsel to do

the questioning: "Mr. Lincoln would tell me what to ask, having reference to some witness on the Norris trial" (*Informants* 22).

46   *The prosecution's case*: My description of this is carefully based on all available records, mostly the original court documents. The presentation here could easily have been lengthened, the detail made more numerous, had I been willing to press the more ephemeral implications of the documents. But there's a limit, and I prefer to stop on the near side. It is certainly true, at any rate, that the leading impression made by the prosecution on the jurors would have been very strong indeed. The juror Brady said as much (Gridley 40).

Fullerton's having Allen stand up and demonstrate the blow is from Duff's own statement that *Lincoln* asked the witness on cross-examination "to tell how it was done. He got up and went through the motion, struck an overhand blow, just as he declared he saw me do" (Barton 514). Duff's brother Asbury, who attended the trial as a seventeen-year-old, also recalled that "Allen in describing the encounter in court illustrated the manner in which Duff delivered his blows . . . raising his right hand as high as his face, and striking an overhand blow" (Gridley 43). The two statements refer to what was done by Lincoln, but surely Fullerton would have thought of it too.

47   "be cleared before sundown"—Hannah Armstrong in her statement to Herndon (*Informants* 526). She doesn't note just when during the day Lincoln said this, leaving writers free to judge where it might go best, and the conclusions have been several. It is interesting that the juror Brady also recalled hearing Lincoln say this, though he places it at the conclusion of the trial: "As we were leaving the courtroom to pass into the jury room, I heard Mr. Lincoln tell Mrs. Armstrong that her boy would be cleared before sundown, which proved to be true" (Gridley 41). I place it at the most probable juncture, that is, following presentation of the state's case. Putting it at the end of the trial as Brady does radically changes the meaning. There it would properly refer to the possible time to be consumed by the jury deliberations.

48   *The defense witnesses*: How many of the twenty-two actually took the stand isn't known. Nor are any details of their testimony on record. That the eyewitnesses would have been questioned in the manner I show is fairly definite—see the testimony of Nelson Watkins as to their blanket denial that Duff had used a weapon.

48   *Nelson Watkins on the stand*: Gridley 42. My picture of Lincoln
       questioning this witness is formed on the basis of Brady's letter to
       Gridley in which he details the conversation at the Watkins home
       two months after the trial (see above, 113). Watkins' signed travel
       voucher, dated May 8, 1858, for attendance at the Cass County
       court places him in Beardstown for no fewer than six days, May
       3–8, allowing Lincoln further chance to confer on his testimony.
       Lincoln's cutting open the leather casing is in Beveridge 566. The
       same incident was earlier (1912) described by Duff's brother
       John, who was present at the trial. When the slung-shot was pro-
       duced in court, "Mr. Nelson Watkins claimed he had had one that
       he had made by melting and running a mixture of lead and zinc
       into an egg shell and covering it with the leather from a boot leg,
       sewing the leather with a string made of squirrel skin which he
       had tanned. He was placed upon the witness stand by Mr. Lincoln
       and without any opportunity to see or examine the weapon,
       described it perfectly, and before the jury Mr. Lincoln took his
       pocket knife and cut off the covering and found it exactly as
       described" (*Journal of the Lincoln Centennial Association*, Spring-
       field, 1912, 59–60). The sequence and wording of the two sen-
       tences is a bit confused: the first actually describes what happened
       after Watkins took the stand. Obviously there is also disagree-
       ment as to the actual metals involved, lead-zinc or lead-copper.
           I think it can be taken as certain that Watkins, as he claimed,
       was the owner of the slung-shot. But even that point was later
       disputed by the prosecution's co-counsel, Henry Shaw. "It was
       made by Armstrong for the occasion," he wrote some seven years
       after the trial. "He took a common bar of pig lead, pounded it
       round, about the size of a large hickory nut, then cut a piece of
       leather out of the top of one of his boots, & with a thread & nee-
       dle he sewed it into the shape of a slung-shot, & thus improvised
       in a very few minutes a very fatal weapon" (*Informants* 334). Shaw
       gives no proof, and perhaps it wouldn't have been so easy as he
       assumes to make a slung-shot on the spur of the moment. Would
       an angry Duff Armstrong casting about for a weapon to use
       against Metzger have stopped long enough to make one? A length
       of wood was all Norris needed.

50   *Dr. Parker*: In Judge Harriott's opinion it was the Parker testi-
       mony that clinched Duff's acquittal. The "moon theory" and the
       business of the almanac helped, he admitted, but they were not
       the essential things. See above 143.

51 *Charles Allen on the stand*: My picture of Lincoln questioning this witness is based on information supplied by two of the lawyers, Walker and Shaw (*Informants* 22, 316), the juror John Brady (Gridley 39–40), and all that is specified elsewhere, then and later, as to the moon, its position and degree of brightness. Brady's two remarks about Lincoln's technique in the questioning are from his letter in Gridley 40. For a discussion of Allen's distance from the fight see above, 58. In my view the distance was no more than fifty feet, and probably less. Apparently there were trees in the area but these are nowhere mentioned as having been obstacles.

52 "got up and went"—Duff Armstrong's statement: see Appendix C. Same claim by Duff's brother in Gridley 43.

54 *Time of moonset*: In the *Jayne's* almanac for August 29, because moonset came after midnight the designation given is the word "morn." This refers a reader to the morning of the next day, the thirtieth, where moonset is listed as occurring at "0.03." Of course Lincoln in questioning Allen would have used a simpler, more forceful way of making his point.

 Attorney Walker ineptly clouds the issue by some unconsidered remarks in 1866 to Herndon, *seeming* to say that at the time of the fight the moon had set : "We showed by the almanac that at the hour of 11 at night no moon was visible, and by other witnesses that at the time of the trouble it was quite dark" (*Informants* 326). Actually, he is simply claiming for Armstrong what he'd already claimed (unsuccessfully) for Norris, that the moon was *too low* in the heavens to sufficiently light the scene of the crime. Carelessly he uses unqualified terms ("no moon was visible . . . quite dark") to mean something much less absolute.

54 *The Almanac*: For determining the precise manner in which this item was introduced and used by Lincoln at the trial, the primary materials, barely sufficient to start with, are not a little confused. Basic are the letters by attorney Shaw (*Informants* 316), and the juror Brady (Gridley 40), also a detailed statement in Bergen (393), and a shorter one in the paper by Mrs. Schweer (Gridley 26). Brief references are also made by the attorney Walker and Judge Harriott (*Informants* 325–26, 703). Analyzing all these against a background of court procedure, and common sense, gives the sequence I provide. That the booklet-almanac was in fact a *Jayne's* I accept on the word of jury foreman Logan, reported by Shaw (*Informants* 316), reported also in an affidavit made by Logan (Bergen 393). In addition to the latitude of

Philadelphia, *Jayne's* also gave astronomical data for the latitude of Boston, moonset there on August 29 occurring at 11:51, twelve minutes ahead of the lower latitude. *Ayer's* gives calculations for both the Boston and New York latitudes.

None of the three almanacs is as rare today as has been believed (though a *Goudy's* for 1857 still eludes my search). More than a dozen institutions around the country have special collections of American almanacs, many including one or another of the three named in the Armstrong case. My own gratitude for supplying photocopies of various items goes to Alexander Library, Rutgers University, and Lilly Library, Indiana University.

One tangential incident in the courtroom relating to the almanac as introduced by Lincoln I have not covered in the narrative, nor has any other writer picked it up. It is a brief but quite confusing incident that was reported only by the juror John Brady. Supposedly, after Lincoln quoted from the *Jayne's*, Fullerton rose and corrected him: "Mr. Lincoln, you are mistaken. The moon was just coming up instead of going down at that time." To this, says Brady, Lincoln replied that either way it served his purpose since the moon "was not overhead as Mr. Allen swore it was" (Gridley 40). Whatever led Fullerton to venture such a contradictory comment is not explained, but it quite obviously rested on a simple misreading of the almanac. In the *Jayne's* the moon column is headed "Moon Rises," seeming to apply to the column as a whole. Reading carefully down, however, it is seen that the *Rises* becomes *Sets* as the month progresses, and is so plainly marked. A hurried reading might easily miss the switch in the small, crowded type. That Lincoln corrected his corrector is very probable, though he could also have added the comment quoted by Brady as insurance against any last-minute disturbance in the minds of the jurymen.

Confusion of that sort is a thread running through many of the sources, a main cause of much of the later contradiction and distortion. To illustrate, take Shaw's 1866 letter. He writes that Lincoln—before the trial began but presumably the same day—gave an almanac to the court clerk, "stating that he might call for one during the trial, & if he did to send him that one." But when eventually Lincoln requested the almanac, "two were brought, one of the year of the murder, the other of the year previous." With that, Shaw then proceeds to tangle things still further by reporting the claim of the Cass County sheriff, James Dick, "who says that he saw a *Goudy's* almanac laying upon Mr. Lincoln's table during the trial, & that Mr. Lincoln took it out of his own pocket" (*Informants* 316).

Judge Bergen supplies a more sensible note when he says that, rather than procuring an almanac in Beardstown, Lincoln, "with his usual care, had brought with him from Springfield the almanac then regarded as standard in the region." He adds another comment involving procedure which is interesting if uncertain. Even before questioning Allen, says Bergen, Lincoln formally submitted the almanac to the judge to have it admitted in evidence, "in order that there might be no question as to its subsequent use" (Bergen 393). Since this move would have tipped the prosecution to what was coming, perhaps Bergen is here mistaken. In any case, he then proceeds to cloud the matter still further by stating that "at a recess of the court he took it [the almanac] from his capacious hat and gave it to sheriff Dick with the request that he would hand it to him when he called for it" (Bergen 394).

The only detail in my depiction of this action that I'd be willing to reconsider concerns the possibility that Lincoln gave the three copies into the care of the court clerk, rather than keeping them in his briefcase. Whether that is true or not, I also think it probable that the clerk *did* at some point, for some reason, hand a different almanac to Lincoln, one he'd found elsewhere in the courthouse or fetched from outside—perhaps it was the *Goudy's* seen by Sheriff Dick. Of course, this whole question is closely tied up with the later charges about a faked almanac, which takes the confusion to still another level: for further discussion see chapter five and Notes. Here, it is only necessary to enforce the undoubted fact that the almamac used by Lincoln in court that day was legitimate, authentic, and completely undoctored. See also two notes down.

55   "roar of laughter"—*Informants* 316

55   "floored"—Mentioned by Shaw in his letter of 1866 after speaking with several members of the jury (*Informants* 16). All readily recalled how badly Allen had been shaken by Lincoln's quoting from the slim volume, agreeing that "the almanac *floored* the witness" (italics in original). Shaw's real purpose in talking with these men was to hear what they might have to say about the

almanac itself, but seemingly they didn't help him much there. That Lincoln terminated his questioning of Allen at this point is my own conclusion.

55   *Fullerton sending for an almanac*: Bergen 393, which also describes the hurried conference which followed. That someone, no doubt a clerk, perhaps more than one, actually left the courtroom in search of an almanac, of course to check on Lincoln, seems to be a fact, so it isn't strange that differing reasons and persons were later assigned to the action. Besides Judge Bergen, at least two others mention it. Walker recalled that an almanac was brought in "from some one of the clerk's offices below," adding that it was done "at my request" (*Informants* 325). In 1909 Duff's brother Asbury told Mrs. Schweer that Lincoln "asked a cousin of Armstrong, John Jakes by name, to go out and get him an almanac at the nearest store" (quoted in Gridley 26 from the Schweer paper). Of course, whether it was cousin Jake or anyone else who went out hunting for an almanac, it was *not* Lincoln who sent him. In the minutes after he cited the almanac, I conclude finally there was a *general* hubbub in court with several people calling for other, different almanacs.

58   *Moon experiments*: The changeableness of the moon in location and appearance according to the position of the observer is an effect little noticed or discussed—*never* in the Armstrong case. One sharp observer of such lunar gymnastics is Robert Frost, whose little poem "The Freedom of the Moon" nicely catches the possibilities. It seems he was accustomed, as he walked along some country road, to moving the moon around at will, making a little game of it. Besides altering its location he also notes how size and brightness are affected.

The moon's natural movements in the night sky, caused by a shifting earthly sight-line, he pretends to have in his control. In the poem's opening he pictures the moon as a jewel a woman ties in her hair, alone or with other ornaments such as a star. He notes the change of lustre in relation to the surroundings. Of course his interest is whimsically artistic not legal, but the result is the same, demonstrating the dramatic alterations possible. He concludes:

> I put it shining anywhere I please.
> By walking slowly on some evening later,

I've pulled it from a crate of crooked trees,
And brought it over glossy water, greater,
And dropped it in, and seen the image wallow,
The color run, all sorts of wonder follow.

60   *Fullerton's summation*: There is no record of this, but its elements, I think, are obvious, particularly his trying to turn Lincoln's use of the almanac back on him. I also feel sure that he went at it in much fuller and more specific fashion than I describe.

61   "When he rose to speak"—Herndon 331–32.

62   "The last 15 minutes"—*Informants* 22.
    "No contract. Not"—Herndon 276. Same for the next quotation in this paragraph.

63   "It came Lincoln's turn"—Bergen 392.

64   "he removed his coat"—Gridley 40. That the day was hot and the crowded courtroom sultry are reasons often given for Lincoln divesting himself for the closing argument. The obvious question is why he waited so long—till he was approaching the jury—to do so, why he sat all day in the courtroom fully clothed.

66   "backwoodsy"—Gridley 41.

66   "fiery eloquence"—Gridley 41. The juror Brady affords quite a good illustration of how very effective was Lincoln's strategy with regard to Allen and the almanac. Says Brady: "I am satisfied that the jury thought Allen was telling the truth. I know that he impressed me that way, but his evidence with reference to the moon was so far from the facts that it destroyed his evidence with the jury . . . the almanac showed that the moon at that time was going out of sight, setting" (Gridley 40). But of course Lincoln in lowering the moon from where Allen said it was, had not at all proved the absence of sufficient light, though that is certainly the impression he hoped to create.

67   "He told of his kind"—*Informants* 22.

67   "He told the jury of"—*Informants* 316.

68   "He took the jury by"—*Informants* 336.

68   "Such was the power"—*Informants* 22.

68   "Tears were plentifully"—Gridley 41.

71   *Instructions to the jury*: These are quoted from the originals, apparently in the hand of Judge Harriott. The manuscript of Lincoln's suggested addition, two paragraphs, is preserved at the Illinois State Historical Society, Springfield. It is the only document

from the Armstrong trial written by Lincoln, and is unsigned. Nothing else bears his signature, either.

72   *The jury deliberations*: Juror Brady is the only source for this aspect of the trial: "We were out less than an hour; only one ballot was taken and that was unanimous for acquittal" (Gridley 40). If the ballot was without disagreement, and but a single ballot taken, what occupied the hour?

72   "We the jury acquit"—Quoted from the written verdict, signed by jury foreman Milton Logan. Unlike the Norris verdict, the other eleven jurors did not add their signatures.

72   *Hannah Armstrong*: That she did not return to the courtroom to hear the verdict is in her 1866 interview: "I went down to Thompson's pasture. Staton came and told me soon that my son was cleared—and a free man. I went up to the courthouse—the Jury shook hands with me—so did the Court—so did Lincoln. We were all affected and tears streamed down Lincoln's eyes"(*Informants* 526).

Chapter Four: The One Who Went to Jail

73   *The Norris letter to Lincoln*: From the original in the Lincoln Collection, Library of Congress. I am grateful to John Lupton of the Lincoln Legals who called the letter to my attention. Note that "Mr. W. Haines of Havana" was also one of the men called in the Armstrong trial as a *prosecution* witness, a curious fact; see above, 143.

78   *Yates and Greene*: The relationships between Yates and Lincoln, and Greene and Lincoln, are well known, that between Greene and Yates less so, but it was equally close. That Yates headed the Tonica and Petersburg Railroad is also a known fact, but not Greene's replacing him in the position. That fact is stated in the *Chicago Tribune*, July 11, 1860, and the letterhead of his note to Yates confirms it: specifying four officers of the company, it names Greene as president (see also Miller 712–13). By then Greene and Yates had known each other for many years. "When I was in Illinois College," wrote Greene later, "I brought home with me, one vacation, my young friend Dick Yates, present Republican candidate for governor, and some other boys" (Mearns I, 154).

78   "I am not personally"—from the original letter in the pardon files of the Illinois State Archives, Springfield. The name Pelham

occurs in the 1860 Census for Menard County but I have not found a William. The signatures of five Pelhams are on the pardon petition.

How Greene's part in the pardon scheme was arranged can only be suggested: through Herndon in person at Lincoln's old Springfield law office, all parties avoiding any written statements and instructions. Interestingly, however, it is also possible that the initial contact with Greene was made directly by Lincoln himself. During 1861 (the specific day is not known) Greene actually was a visitor to the White House, apparently by invitation, where he was warmly greeted and shown around by Lincoln. At one point Lincoln introduced him to Secretary of State William Seward as the man who had taught him grammar back in New Salem days (Tarbell 140, Walsh 62, 155). For what it is worth another little-known fact should be noted here: sometime the next year (1862) Lincoln appointed Greene Collector of Internal Revenue for northern Illinois.

79   "Mr. Pelham, a citizen"—from the original in the pardon files of the Illinois State Archives, Springfield. It is simply impossible, of course, that Herndon would have been involved in this matter had not Lincoln personally asked for his help. Herndon's sparse knowledge of the actual case, however, shows that even at this juncture Lincoln did not tell him more than was necessary—leaving Herndon free in conscience to write later that his old partner would never "sacrifice truth or right in the slightest degree for the love of a friend" (Herndon 484).

79   *The Pardon petition*: The original of this four-page document, unpublished and till now unnoticed, is in the pardon files of the Illinois State Archives, Springfield. Its effort to impugn the testimony of the main prosecution witness, Charles Allen, was routine, in this case much bolstered by Allen's repudiation at the Beardstown trial. This fact and the wording and approach in general sufficiently identifies it as from the hand of a lawyer, who is not named.

83   "Generalships in the"—Lincoln, *Works* V, 186.

83   *Letter of Norris to Yates*: from the original in the pardon files of the Illinois State Archives, Springfield. Norris' calling the attorney Walker "a young man inexperienced at the bar," wasn't quite true. At the time of the trial Walker was thirty-eight years old, with an established law practice in Havana, Mason County. Norris' focusing on Allen's testimony while ignoring that of Watkins and

Parker of course is understandable. Whether he understood that the evidence offered by the latter two actually made his own guilt more certain would be interesting to know.

85   *Letter of Walker to Yates*: From the original in the pardon files of the Illinois State Archives, Springfield. It is my own conclusion that Walker wrote at the invitation of Yates, but I do not insist on it. Whatever, or whoever, prompted Norris to write Yates could also have activated Walker. At a guess I would choose Herndon, again acting for Lincoln.

86   "Please issue pardon"—From the original in the pardon files of the Illinois State Archives, Springfield. Norris' release from prison is noted in the penitentiary's *seventh annual report*, 1863–64, p. 44, which says he was equipped with "five dollars cash and clothing of the value of fifteen dollars" (Duff 359).

86   *The Lincoln Papers*: For the story of this collection see Mearns, vol. 1. The unsealing of the papers fifty years ago, as Mearns shows (135–36), was an event of extraordinary public interest. Perhaps part of the reason why the Norris letter lay unnoticed for so long was the sheer bulk of the collection, almost two hundred large folio volumes crammed with documents large and small. Still, soon after the unsealing an index was made available containing almost forty thousand entries.

Chapter Five: The Faked Almanac

89   *Source of the charge*: Judge Bergen in the 1890s was fairly precise in tracing the story's first appearance in print to one of the Armstrong jurors, never named. Sometime in 1860, he recalls,

> I saw in a Democratic newspaper, published at St. Louis, an article personally abusive of Mr. Lincoln, saying he was no statesman, only a third-rate lawyer, and to prove the deception and dishonest nature of the candidate, printed an indefinite affidavit of one of the jurors who had acquitted Armstrong that Mr. Lincoln made fraudulent use of an almanac in the trial. He seems not to have called this—his pretended knowledge—to the attention of the other jurors, but very promptly joined in the verdict of acquittal, and would seem not to have known or remembered that there was anything wrong till during a heated political canvas (Bergen 393).

That the story of a doctored almanac was in circulation by word of mouth well before 1860 is shown by Henry Shaw's reference to it as being widely rumored in Beardstown and adjacent areas at the time of the trial (*Informants* 316). He actually calls it the "prevailing belief," which seems a bit overstated. That the charge was leveled during Lincoln's senatorial campaign of 1858 is stated in many sources but I have not been able to document it—though perhaps proof is hardly needed. If, following the trial in May 1858, such a damning charge really was in circulation, then it would surely have been picked up and used by the Douglas forces even before Lincoln's nomination for the senatorship in mid-June.

Today's sensibilities often miss the very serious nature of this charge of legal fraud. By itself it could easily have been sufficient to derail a candidacy, not to mention bringing criminal charges. To my mind, the fact that the Douglas campaign didn't do more with it is still another proof of the legend's lack of substance. There is no doubt that Douglas' supporters closely examined every lead of this sort. If they could have established it as more than rumor, they would surely have splashed it across every available newspaper, and Douglas himself would have used it in the debates as well as his dozens of other speeches during the campaign of 1858.

90   "it is easy to pervert"—Lamon 328.

91   "of the year previous"—*Informants* 316. Same for the other two quotations in this paragraph. Concerning Logan's affidavit, which has been lost, Judge Bergen says: "Soon afterwards I saw an affidavit by Milton Logan, the foreman of the jury, that he personally examined the almanac, when handed to the jury, and particularly noticed that it was for 1857, the year of the homicide" (Bergen 393).

91   "Into a drug store"—Lucas.

92   "confidently point out"—Barton 511.

92   "An almanac is in"—Barton 312–13. Same for the other two quotations in this paragraph. The Armstrong case, complains Barton, "has attained a prominence greater than it deserves," and then he proceeds to devote nearly twenty pages to a discussion of it (half in his text, half in an appendix). By the time his biography of Lincoln was published (1925) he explains (315) that the spurious almanac so painstakingly examined by him had "disappeared" from the files of the Chicago Historical Society. Judging by what

Barton says of it, this particular fake wasn't a very good example of the forger's art. The collector who got stung—to the tune of a mere fifty dollars—was a certain Mr. Gunther of Chicago. He bought it from the man who handled the auction of the deceased Shaw's books and papers. Later, Shaw's executor, on hearing of the supposed faked almanac, first denied that there had been an almanac of any sort in the Shaw estate. Then he confronted the man who'd sold it: "In a hesitating way he answered that he had found the almanac [among Shaw's papers] and had sold it to some person in New York, but could not give me the purchaser's name" (Barton 313).

94   *Moonset in early biographies*: Lamon 329, Gridley 26–27, Barton 313, 315, Beveridge 571.

95   "Nearly the extreme"—Olson and Doescher 188. The two physicists, Donald Olson and Russell Doescher, are on the staff of the physics department, Southwest Texas State University, San Marcos, Texas. Following a few older accounts of the case they call the site of the crime "Virgin's Grove," rather than Walker's. Both names refer to the same place, William Virgin having acquired it some years later. Their article offers an illustration of what a "waxing, gibbous moon," would have looked like, being "74-percent sunlit." Old weather records, they add, show that the night of August 29, 1857 was a fairly balmy one: "a temperature of 56 degrees Fahrenheit, a light breeze from the northwest, and completely clear skies."

Of special interest is a chart they provide showing the progress of the moon that night from rising to setting. It crossed the meridian at Walker's Grove at 7:44 P.M., and by the hour of the fight, 11 P.M., it had declined to 8 degrees altitude, 221 degrees azimuth. The description by the witness Charles Allen of the moon being nearly overhead at the time of the fight would place it where it actually was at about 9 P.M., some two hours off. How Allen made this mistake isn't hard to understand, given the imprecise physical and visual reltions between a hurried observer's position on the ground, and a large bright object in the night sky. Also, of course, Allen's whole attention was on the fight in progress. Only weeks or months later was he required to state exactly *where* the moon had been, how high up. Anyone's memory in such a situation—the strong, sharp contrast between light and dark—could well make an error of an hour or two in the moon's position.

97   *No challenge by Fullerton*: Beveridge, in his excellent Lincoln biography, has a lengthy discussion of the Armstrong case (in my view the most factually reliable, so far as it goes in depending on the then existing documents, among all previous treatments). Talking of Lincoln's use of the almanac, he says quite correctly that it was not the stroke of legal genius it is often pictured, for "any alert lawyer could not possibly have failed to do the same thing; thousands of resourceful lawyers have devised other expedients equally skillful to impair or break down positive testimony" (571). Of course this is true, and in reverse fashion it applies as well to prosecutor Fullerton, the widely experienced state's attorney. Faced with the evidence of Lincoln's almanac, Fullerton could not possibly have failed to test it against other almanacs, so that the absence of a challenge by him is proof positive that he found nothing untoward to challenge.

97   "Uncle Johnny Potter"—Barton 509. An old New Salemite, Potter knew Lincoln well and was an eyewitness of the famous wrestling match.

98   *Surviving almanacs*: Barton states that "local tradition" (1925) identifies an *Ayer's* as the one used by Lincoln (contradicting jury foreman Logan who said it was a *Jayne's*). The Ayer's firm, adds Barton, was sure that Lincoln used their product, and sent him photos of the relevant pages made from "the only copy of the almanac which the firm has" (315). Today, however, copies of the *Ayer's*, as well as the other two almanacs mentioned in the case are held by any number of institutions in special collections of both American and foreign publications.

99   "Here, Henry, I'll give"—*Informants* 334.

Epilogue: Snapshots

101   *The Byers photograph*: Hamilton 14–15, Lorant 117. The original is now at the University of Nebraska, donated by Byers' widow.

103   *Duff Armstrong*: For his marriages, his army service, illness, and discharge by Lincoln, see *Hannah Armstrong Wilcox Materials* at the Lincoln Library (Sanagamon Room), Springfield. While Duff seldom talked of his trial, he always carried with him Lincoln's brief note to his mother about the discharge, often showing it to friends and drinking companions (Masters 156).

104   "I have just ordered"—Lincoln, *Complete Works*, VI, 462. The

original of the note is now at Brown University. That it is a letter in Lincoln's own hand is clear. Some sources refer to it as a telegram.

104   *Hannah Armstrong*: Her death was briefly noted in the *Winterset News*, August 21, 1890, without reference to Lincoln: "Mrs. Wilcox, mother of Robert Armstrong, of this city, died Tuesday. She was an old lady and well known in this county where she had hundreds of friends. The body was taken to Ashland, Illinois, her old home for burial on the Wednesday morning train." Ashland, Illinois, at that time was where her son Duff had his home.

106   *The Beardstown kick-off*: Baringer 224. Additional information was kindly supplied by Michael Bonansinga, mayor of Beardstown. The platform from which Lincoln spoke would have been even nearer the courthouse, in the same block, had not Douglas spoken there the day before. Republicans didn't want their man using the same site as the Democrat.

107   "a pugilistic encounter"—*Works*, II, 541. Same for the next quotation in this paragraph.

107   "playing *two upon one*"—*Works*, II, 543.

107   "Among the old men"—*Works*, II, 543.

108   "bespattered with every"—*Works*, III, 334. There exists no separate or extensive study of the 1858 campaign overall. The interest is mostly in the seven debates with Douglas, though Lincoln delivered at least sixty speeches, Douglas more than a hundred. There was extensive newspaper coverage of the entire campaign (see Harper 21-26), but no one has yet undertaken to hunt for occurrences of the faked almanac charge (no surprise, since it involves staring at a vast waste of newspaper print on miles of microfilm). Yet in the small type and crowded columns of Democratic papers for both 1858 and 1860 must lurk at least a few apparently damning stories about a doctored almanac.

SELECTED BIBLIOGRAPHY

Listed here are published sources, those named in the text or the Notes, with a few items which supplied background information. For description and comment on the original legal documents cited in text or Notes, including the Norris pardon file, see pp. 4, 129, 161.

Angle, P., *Lincoln*, 1854–1861, Springfield, MA, 1935.

Armstrong, J., "Remarks," *Lincoln Centennial Assoc. Journal*, 1912.

Baringer, W., *Lincoln Day by Day* 1849–1860, Washington, 1960.

Barrett, J., *Life of Abraham Lincoln*, New York, 1865.

Barton, W., *Life of Abraham Lincoln*, Indianapolis, IN, 1925.

Bergen, A., "Lincoln as a Lawyer," *Journal of the American Bar association*, V. 12, June 1926.

Beveridge, A., *Abraham Lincoln* 1809–1858, Boston, 1928.

Burlingame, M., *The Inner World of Abraham Lincoln*, Urbana, IL, 1994.

Davis, C., *In Search of the Missing Lincoln* (pamphlet), Lincoln Legal Papers Project, Springfield, MA, 1994.

Donald, D., *Lincoln*, New York, 1995

Duff, J., *A. Lincoln: Prairie Lawyer*, New York, 1960.

East, E., "The Melissa Goings Murder Case," *Journal of the Illinois Historical Society*, Spring 1953.

Fehrenbacher, D., *Prelude to Greatness: Lincoln in the 1850s*, Stanford, 1962.

———, *Recollected Words of Abraham Lincoln*, Stanford, 1996.

Ferguson, D., "Story of the Almanac used by Lincoln in the Armstrong trial," *Journal of the Illinois State Historical Society*, Vol 15, No. 3, 1937.

Frank, J., *Lincoln As a Lawyer*, Urbana, IL, 1961.

Gridley, J., "Lincoln's Defense of Duff Armstrong," *Journal of the Illinois Historical Society*, April 1910.

Hamilton, J., and Ostendorf, L., *Lincoln in Photographs*, Norman, OK, 1985.

Harper, R., *Lincoln and the Press*, New York, 1951.

Herndon, W., *Herndon's Lincoln: The True Story of a Great Life*, Chicago, 1889; repr. Da Capo Press, 1983.

Hertz, E., *The Hidden Lincoln*, New York, 1938

Hill, F., *Lincoln the Lawyer*, New York, 1906.

Hodges, C., "Lawyer Lincoln for the Defense," *King Features Syndicate*, 1958.

King, J., "Lincoln's Skill As a Lawyer," *North American Review*, February 1898.

Lamon, W., *The Life of Abraham Lincoln from his Birth to his Inauguration as President*, Boston, 1872.

Lincoln. A., *Collected Works*, ed. Roy Basler et al., 8 vols., New Brunswick, NJ, 1953.

Lorant, S., "A Day in the Life of Abraham Lincoln," *Life Magazine*, February 10, 1948.

Lucas, A., "Did Duff Armstrong Kill Metzger?" *Daily Illinoian-Star*, July 6, 1929.

Luthin, R., *The Real Lincoln*, Englewood Cliffs, NJ, 1960.

Masters, E., "Days in the Lincoln Country," *Journal of the Illinois Historical Society*, Vol. 18, February 1926.

———, "Dreiser at Spoon River," *Esquire*, May 1939.

Mearns, D., *The Lincoln Papers*, 2 vols, Garden City, NY, 1948.

Miller, R., *History of Menard and Mason Counties*, Chicago, 1879.

Neely, M., Jr., *The Lincoln Encyclopedia*, New York, 1982.

Olson, D., and Doescher, R., "Lincoln and the Almanac Trial," *Sky and Telescope*, August 1990.

Onstot, T., *Pioneers of Menard and Mason Counties*, Chicago, 1902.

Perrin, H., *History of Cass County, Illinois*, Chicago, 1882.

Reep, T., *Lincoln at New Salem*, Petersburg, IL, 1927.

Rowland, R, and Rowland, S., *Clary Geneology*, Fairfield, VA, 1980.

Tarbell, I., "Lincoln as a Lawyer," *McClure's*, July 1896.

Thomas, B., *Lincoln's New Salem*, Carbondale, IL, 1954, 1987.

Townsend, W., "Lincoln's Defense of Duff Armstrong," *Journal of the American Bar Assoc.*, Feb. 1925.

Wheeler, B., "Lincoln Repays a New Salem Friend," *Hobbies*, (Chicago, April 1948.

Wilson, D., *Honor's Voice: The Transformation of Abraham Lincoln*, New York, 1998.

Wilson, D., and Davis, R., *Herndon's Informants: Letters, Interviews, and Statements about Abraham Lincoln*. Urbana, IL, 1998.

Woldman, A., *Lawyer Lincoln*, Boston, 1936.

Walsh, J., *The Shadows Rise: Abraham Lincoln and the Ann Rutledge Legend*, Urbana, IL, 1993.

ACKNOWLEDGMENTS

For historians of Lincoln's law career these are palmy days. All the arduous and time-consuming work of researching the original documents of his cases has now been done for them by the extraordinary Lincoln Legals Project of Springfield ("A Documentary History of the Law Practice of Abraham Lincoln, 1836–1861"). For the original papers connected with any of the literally thousands of cases handled by Lincoln in his twenty-six years at the Illinois bar, often including trial proceedings, the Lincoln Legals can supply both basic information and copies of original documents, all gathered from dusty archives in dozens of old courthouses across Illinois.* On top of that, the staff of the Project is made up of a willing, informed, and cheerfully helpful set of friendly experts! I here record my own indebtedness to them for information and for copies of the original documents in the Armstrong case, especially Director Cullom Davis, Martha Benner, and John Lupton. Of course they are not to be held accountable for the

---

* As of February 2000 the entire archive is available on DVD from the University of Illinois Press.

use I make of these documents, or for any of the interpretations and conclusions herein.

My grateful thanks go also to the staffs of various accommodating libraries: The Wisconsin State Historical Society, Madison; Memorial Library, University of Wisconsin, Madison; The New York Public Library at 42nd Street; Dixon Homestead Library, Dumont, New Jersey. In Beardstown I was kindly aided by Alice Schnake, public library; Nancy Lamb, City Hall, Sally Lael, the Beardstown *Star-Register*, and Michael Bonansinga, Mayor; in Havana by Joann Lynn; in Springfield by George Hermann, Illinois State Historical Society, William Kohlmyer, Illinois State Archives, Linda Garvert, Sangamon Room, Lincoln Public Library, and Herschel Armstrong.

For various sorts of timely aid, now and over the years, my thanks go to my wife Dorothy, my daughter Ann (Mrs. William Marriott), my son Matthew who took time out of a busy life to read the manuscript and offer helpful comment, and sons Timothy and John, always ready to assist.

INDEX